W9-CPF-374

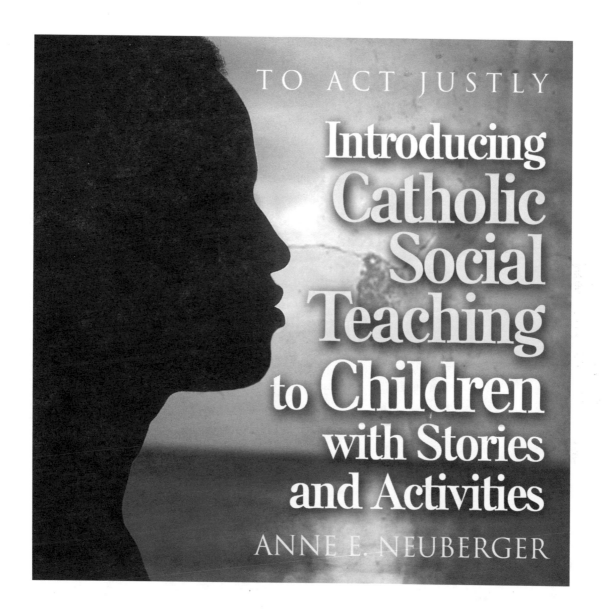

TO ACT JUSTLY

Introducing Catholic Social Teaching to Children with Stories and Activities

ANNE E. NEUBERGER

TWENTY-THIRD PUBLICATIONS

185 WILLOW STREET • PO BOX 180 • MYSTIC, CT 06355
TEL: 1-800-321-0411 • FAX: 1-800-572-0788
E-MAIL: ttpubs@aol.com • www.twentythirdpublications.com

Bayard

Dedication

To Edward Flahavan and Jerry McMullen

and all the people of Saint Stephen's parish,
including those who now float lightly among the rafters.

You have already been told what is right
and what Yahweh wants of you.
Only this, to act justly, to love tenderly,
and to walk humbly with your God.
—Micah 6:8

Ackowledgments

The author would like to thank the following people for their assistance in bringing this book about:
Dunia Berganza Ruff, Alison Berger, Gwen Costello, Linda Hanson, Jane Hilger, Sr. Jeanne Houlihan,
Sandy Knauff, Ron Krietemeyer, Paul Marincel, and Deborah Ruddy.

Twenty-Third Publications
A Division of Bayard
185 Willow Street
P.O. Box 180
Mystic, CT 06355
(860) 536-2611
(800) 321-0411
www.twentythirdpublications.com

ISBN:1-58595-222-2.
Library of Congress Catalog Card Number: 2002103866
Printed in the U.S.A.

Contents

Part III: Exploring the Principles of Catholic Social Teaching

Part IV: Resources for Action

INTRODUCTION

All the great religions of the world teach that faith demands justice. Christianity's call to a strong social justice tradition has its roots in the Jewish Scriptures. In Exodus, we are told God hears the cry of the poor and oppressed. The great prophet Isaiah teaches us "the way to lasting peace is to work for justice." Micah counsels us to "live justly, love tenderly, and walk humbly with your God."

Then Jesus came to us, with his tremendous compassion for those who suffer. Through his teachings, particularly the beatitudes, he showed us how to be compassionate. His own call to justice meant dying on the cross.

The early Christians did much to work against the injustices of their day, providing help to those who were hungry, sick, and orphaned. Centuries later, Catholic social justice was still being carried out, now in European monasteries where monks provided education, medical care, shelter, and food to those in need.

The challenges brought about by the Industrial Revolution called for a broadening approach to social justice. The change from a basically agricultural life to an urban industrial one resulted in overcrowding, exploitation, poverty, and hazardous and unhealthy conditions in the cities. The Catholic Church responded. Bishops called for social reforms, welfare societies were begun in parishes, religious orders opened schools and hospitals. Pope Leo XIII's papal letter *Rerum Novarum*, written in 1891, called for gradual social reform and just wages for workers, and criticized extremes in both socialism and capitalism.

This was the starting point for modern Catholic social teaching. It has been evolving ever since, with the guidance of Leo's successors, and challenged repeatedly by world-shattering events such as worldwide wars, economic depression, and political terrorism. In the early 1960s, Pope John XXIII called for the Second Vatican Council, which resulted in decrees, declarations, and, most significantly, constitutions. One of the four constitutions, *The Church in the Modern World*, gave the Catholic Church a new way to look at the world, the needs of its peoples, and the Church's role in those needs.

Since then, with the support of many bishops, these teachings have been summed up in "The Seven Principles of Catholic Social Teaching," to more easily bring this topic to consciousness and practice. All Catholics are called to act upon these principles, on both an individual and community level.

This makes the principles an essential part of Catholic education. It seems even more imperative that we develop in our children compassion and a desire to help others as this vast world of ours becomes a "global village." The upcoming generation will need to think, feel, and act with a global awareness, for the interconnectedness of the earth's many and varied peoples is becoming more and more a justice issue.

1

Growing Up Catholic in the Midst of Affluence
Why We Need this Book

Children in the United States grow up in the midst of affluence. This does not mean that all these children are affluent. In fact, one in every five children in this country is poor. Poor children, however, are surrounded by others who have an abundance. The miseries of poverty are intensified by the constant enticement to acquire things, through television, movies, billboards, magazines, and the example of other people. A child deprived of basic needs may feel the lack of frills just as keenly. Justifiable discontent and anger, or resignation and despair, can be the result.

Those children who are more fortunate materially often experience a different sort of poverty, a spiritual one. It is easy to become overindulged by an abundance of food, possessions, activities, and choices.

Children with too great a variety of food develop a dissatisfaction with meals, and find it difficult to be grateful for what is served. Classmates make fun of other children's foods. School lunches are dropped into the garbage. Food, so important to both our physical and social needs, becomes a topic to argue over.

Something similar happens with possessions. Children may show disappointment in gifts instead of receiving them graciously. They may fail to care for what they own, and so waste the resources given them. Having too many things also impacts creativity, depriving children of the joy of making or inventing something. When they do create something, they may see it as inferior to a manufactured item. As a result they long for more things, coerce embarrassed parents to buy more, and look for satisfaction in buying and owning things.

The plethora of activities for children begins when they are babies, and continues on into adulthood. Some children have little time for impromptu play by themselves or with friends. As they move from one activity to the next, they don't take time to appreciate God's beauty, like the intricacies of a snowflake caught on a mitten, or the song of a chickadee. They don't have time to be silly or to read a book. Some play three team sports in one season, while others easily quit one activity to take up another. Neither situation teaches them to make a full commitment to one thing and stick with it. Teachers may be reluctant to assign homework because they know how busy the children are after school, and a learning opportunity is lost. Children are often overtired because of the pace they keep, so they may become sick more easily. Families too busy to eat meals together miss the opportunity to support and appreciate each other, and to pray and learn together.

These lifestyles can result in anxiety and depression in young children. Family counselors have seen an increase in parents seeking help with conflicts that arise over children's activities. And, worst of all, this overindulgence rarely teaches children to care for and give to others. Instead it can cause a lack of interest in or commitment to other people, and bring about an overall feeling of discontent with life, rather like the feeling of having eaten too much fudge!

In short, overindulgence depletes the soul.

All our children, though living different degrees of poverty and wealth, are sisters and brothers— they are one generation of the people of God. Giving those we teach an understanding of Catholic social teaching begins to balance the inequalities among them. Less fortunate children learn that God loves them, that they deserve better lives, and they learn the skills they need to achieve their goals. Children from wealthier homes learn that they too are loved by God and are called to share, to help, to learn, and to love others. Both groups need to learn how to work for social justice.

This generation, more than any preceding it, will be a global people. It is imperative that we adults take the responsibility for teaching our children about youngsters in other parts of the world, whose cultures, beliefs, and needs vary immensely. Many of the stories in this book will introduce children of North America to children in other countries.

The first step in any endeavor is to be able to speak about it. Catholic social teaching enables children to talk about the way things should be, as well as talk about the problems. A passion for doing right by others can begin to grow, and lead to action. In this book, I am attempting to give catechists, parents, and children the tools they need to answer the call to live justly, love tenderly, and walk humbly with their God.

Using This Book

The first section of this book explores the beatitudes from Matthew's Gospel; the second looks at the text of *The Church in the Modern World* from the Second Vatican Council; and the third gives examples of the seven principles of Catholic social teaching. Each section begins with an explanation of the teachings, followed by stories and activities. The material in this book can be used in both educational and home settings.

Each of these stories helps readers apply abstract teachings to real life. Part One, centered on the beatitudes, includes stories about saints, holy people who worked for justice in times past. Children learn about the history of justice work in the Church as well as the variety of ways in which it was accomplished. Preceding each story is a short explanation of the meaning of certain words in the beatitude, which will help adults explain the beatitudes to their youngsters.

Part Two, the section on *The Church in the Modern World*, contains stories based on real and current circumstances, with fictionalized characters. The examples help children acquire a wider view of the world while developing a spirit of empathy.

Part Three, the Seven Principles of Catholic Social Teaching, provides stories about real people, mainly from the recent past. These people have been catalysts for justice, bringing about a better world. They can serve as role models to children, and inspire youngsters to act justly in their own lives.

Part Four provides information and ideas for actions or projects pertaining to social justice.

PART ONE

Exploring Jesus' Teachings

Stories of Saints Who Lived the Beatitudes

Introduction

The beatitudes (Matthew 5:1–12) are some of Jesus' most important teachings, the essence of what Jesus continuously taught his disciples. Still, it can be difficult to apply them to our own lives. Stories about people who understood and lived them are helpful. In this section, we will explore each beatitude through the story of a saint whose life exemplified that particular beatitude.

Jesus spoke in Aramaic, and this and the Hebrew language have a common expression, "O the blessedness of...." It is a literary form found in the Old Testament, proclaiming the happiness of a person. In the beatitudes Jesus was not stating what he hoped would come to be, but was confirming what already exists—a blessedness here and now. The beatitudes are not disconcerting instructions, but joyful statements of what we already possess. This joy cannot be taken from us by change or tragedy, for it is an inner happiness from God that transcends everything earthly.

Using Part One

Before beginning these stories, you may want to read with your children the scriptural form of the beatitudes in chapter five of the Gospel of Matthew, in the Sermon on the Mount. A picture Bible can help youngsters visualize Jesus teaching the crowd of people.

Preceding each story is an explanation of the beatitude the story focuses on, to help you discuss the meaning of Jesus' words. After the story you'll find two activities designed to help children apply the beatitude more concretely to their lives. The first activity is for grades two and three, the second for grades four through six. However, usually both can be easily adapted to accommodate any age group. (Information for greater involvement in justice issues can be found in Part Four.)

Following the activities is a brief paragraph with additional information about the saint whose life is highlighted in the story.

When you have completed the beatitude section, invite the children to write their own prayers, asking for God's help in learning about injustices, and asking for guidance. Perhaps these prayers can be read at Mass or printed in the parish bulletin.

A Story of Saint Katharine Drexel

Blessed are the poor in spirit, for theirs is the kingdom of heaven.
—Matthew 5:3

In this beatitude, Jesus is not speaking of physical poverty, but a poverty that leads us to trust in God. Saint Katharine Drexel, though a wealthy woman, teaches by her example how to be "poor in spirit." In Hebrew, a word for "poor" is *ebion*. This word evolved to mean a person who is materially poor, therefore having no power and prestige, and so subject to oppression. With no earthly resources, such persons put their whole trust in God. They become detached from things, and completely attached to God. However, Jesus was not praising physical poverty; in fact, the Christian gospel aims to remove such suffering. Jesus was speaking of poverty of the spirit. Combining the above definition of "poor" with the word "spirit," and using a literary form from the Old Testament, results in a beatitude that can be interpreted as "O the blessedness of those who realize their own helplessness to meet the demands of life, and turn to God for help and strength."

The Story

This story can be told by referring to different years in Saint Katharine's life. You will need seven readers and a sheet of cardboard for each. On one side of the cardboard, write the year (starting with 1858) mentioned in that reader's section. Tape a copy of that section of text onto the back of the cardboard. While the reader holds up the card for the audience to see the year, she/he can read the part.

Reader One	1858: In November of 1858, Katharine Drexel was born into one of the wealthiest families in our country. Like other rich girls, Katharine and her sisters had tutors and were well educated. They danced at balls and traveled to many places. Yet, their parents taught the children to be poor in spirit. The Drexels had a chapel in their home. Every evening, Katharine's father would pray for an hour. Each month, the girls saw their mother pay rent for people who could not afford to. The Drexels gave large amounts of money to charities. They greatly loved their daughters and taught them all about their Catholic faith. They relied on God instead of on their money.
Reader Two	1870: When Katharine was twelve years old, her father bought a summer home. Soon her mother started a Sunday school there for children who were poor, and Katharine was one of the teachers. Her mother devoted two after-

noons a week to working for others who were needy, and Katharine and her sisters helped. During Katharine's teen years, the family traveled all over the United States in their private train car. On one trip, the Drexels saw the great poverty and unhappiness of some Native American people. This upset Katharine greatly. When the family went to Europe, twenty-year-old Katharine was able to meet Pope Leo XIII. She told him about the Native Americans. "Please send people to help them!" Katharine pleaded. She was shocked when the pope said, "Why don't you become a missionary yourself?"

Reader Three	1880: After that, Katharine began to believe that God was calling her not only to share her money, but to give all of herself. Then her mother fell ill, and suffered greatly for three years. Katharine cared for her with love and tenderness. During that difficult time, the young woman continued to experience God's call. After her mother's death, Katharine asked a family friend, Bishop O'Connor, for advice. He said, "Think, pray, and wait." Katherine could have gone anywhere and done anything, but she waited for God to make his will known to her.
Reader Four	1885: When their father died, Katharine and her sisters inherited tremendous wealth. Following what they believed was God's will, the young women focused on the needs of the Native Americans. They traveled around the country, having schools built, and supplying food, clothing, desks, and money for teachers. As they became more aware of the sufferings of African-American people, the Drexels extended their assistance to them as well.
Reader Five	1891: Katharine now knew she wanted to take vows as a religious sister. After learning about the different religious communities, she was advised to start her own order, the Sisters of the Blessed Sacrament. Their mission was to help the poorest people in the United States, the Native Americans and African Americans.
Reader Six	1902: Sister Katharine again traveled the country by train, only now she observed the vow of poverty. She wore threadbare clothing, carried her lunch in a brown paper bag, and bought the cheapest train tickets. And she worked. Over the years, she used her own inherited money, at least twelve million dollars, to start schools. She herself established one hundred and forty-five missions and over sixty schools, in more than sixteen states. One of her greatest accomplishments was starting Xavier University for African Americans. No other university in the southern United States would enroll African Americans because of the segregation laws. All of Katharine's work pointed out the needs of the poor and the evils of injustice.
Reader Seven	1955 and 2000: Sister Katharine Drexel died in 1955, having lived "poor in spirit" for ninety-six years. On October 1, 2000, Katharine Drexel was proclaimed a saint.

Activities

1) When Katharine was a child, she spent two afternoons a week helping others. Name some ways you help other people. Talk with your teacher about more things you can do, perhaps in your school or church.

2) Find out what Katharine's order, the Sisters of the Blessed Sacrament, does now. Try this website: www.katharinedrexel.org

More about This Saint

Saint Katharine's life was remarkable, and she lived in remarkable times. She was born before slavery was abolished, lived through the Indian wars, and died at the dawn of the modern civil rights movement. While her work did not directly challenge the unjust systems, it relieved much suffering, gave dignity to many, and served as a powerful wake-up call to a country whose eyes were closed to the evils of racial prejudice.

A Story of Saint Peter Claver

Blessed are those who mourn, for they shall be comforted.
—Matthew 5:4

In this beatitude Jesus asks us to mourn for our own sins and the sins of the world. One person who lived this beatitude for years was Peter Claver, a man of deep faith and trust in Jesus.

In earlier translations of the beatitudes the Greek word used for "to mourn" is the strongest word for mourning in the Greek language. For example, we find it in the passionate lament of Jacob when he thought his son Joseph was dead. The sorrow of loss comes to everyone. Jesus understood this kind of sorrow, but he may also have been speaking of those who see the suffering of others and suffer with them. Where would we be if such compassion were not a part of this world? Jesus may also have been teaching us about the sorrow we feel at our own sin. When we are faced with sin in all its horror, we can respond by grieving for our part in it.

Knowing this, we might interpret this beatitude as saying, "O the blessedness of those whose hearts are broken by the world's suffering and by personal sin, for from this sorrow will come the joy of forgiveness." Peter Claver lived this beatitude in an exceptional way!

The Story

Read the entire story yourself, or choose four readers for the parts indicated.

Reader One	Cartegna was not a good place to be, yet Peter Claver had left his homeland of Spain to live there. All around him were misery, greed, and evil, for Cartegna was the center of a large slave trade operation. Peter was working against it.
Reader Two	Thousands of African people were kidnapped from their own countries, from their families, and their work. Forced onto ships, they were chained below deck. After two months of starvation and abuse, those who survived the voyage were herded into warehouses like cattle. There they were kept until sold as slaves.
Reader Three	Peter walked through the streets, knowing that most people in the city were connected with this vile business. Hotels were filled with buyers. Offices bustled with salespeople and bookkeepers. Most did not question what they did. For them it was a way of life. A way of death, Peter thought, shouldering a large bag.
Reader Four	Peter was on his way to the docks, where another slave ship had come in.

How many had come in since he arrived? He didn't want to count. Instead, he immersed himself in prayer as he prepared for the ordeal ahead of him. Knowing that Jesus was with him was the only thing that kept him going.

Reader One   Suddenly, a man stepped out in front of him, blocking his way. "Father Claver, I want to speak with you," the well-dressed businessman said. Peter recognized the other man as a landowner, who had many slaves working for him. This man was in town, no doubt to purchase more people to work the vast fields that made him wealthy. "Stay out of the slave business," he said threateningly, stepping closer to Peter. "You are a priest. Your business is with the Church." But Peter answered, "Slavery is wrong. These are children of God, whom you are abusing."

Reader Two   Glaring at Peter, the man backed away. Peter proceeded down the street, burdened by his bag of food and medical supplies. When he reached the dock, he had to persuade the ship's captain to allow him passage onto the ship. All the captains disliked him, yet Peter always convinced each of them to let him on board. Peter knew the Holy Spirit was with him.

Reader Three   As Peter went below deck, he braced himself for the sight and sounds of utter misery. Before him were God's people, bound in chains, hollow with hunger, suffering from wounds, longing for their homes, frightened of what lay before them. Their pain was more than he could bear. But they had no choice, so neither did he. Crying inside, dizzy with anguish, Peter began moving from person to person.

Reader Four   Peter had learned to recognize Africans from different places. He now noticed some who spoke the Poposa language. Perhaps he might find someone today who could interpret for him. This was important, for it respected the captives' dignity. Gently, kindly, he offered water and food to each person. Then he began bandaging wounds and giving medicine.

Reader One   Someday, Peter hoped to tell them about Jesus, but for now he must do what Jesus would do. As he cared for the Africans, he smiled and spoke soothingly, but inside, he was crying out against this injustice. He prayed for those who suffered and for those who caused the suffering.

Reader Two   Squatting beside a young man so weak he could not sit up, Peter gingerly held the man's head up, raising a cup of water to his lips. This man, Peter thought, is Jesus. The suffering of Jesus was all around him.

Reader Three   Peter hoped that eventually slavery would be outlawed. Each person would then be seen as a child of God, and treated with dignity. But for now, Peter cared for each wounded person, suffering with each one of them.

Activities

1) Bring in picture books about Harriet Tubman and Martin Luther King. After reading them, help the children make a timeline. On a long sheet of shelf paper, draw a line starting with the year 1610, when Peter Claver began his work. Make a mark for every ten years and write the year above the line. Continue right up to the current year. Above the year 1850, write in Tubman's name. Above the 1860s, write that slavery was abolished in the United States. Explain that, despite abolition, the former slaves still suffered a great deal. One hundred years later, people like Martin Luther King were still fighting and praying for justice. Above 1960, write King's name. Together, take a good look at the amount of time and misery that has passed. Explain that there is still much prejudice and injustice that injures African Americans today. To mourn as the beatitude says, have some children write prayers for those who suffered during the years between Peter Claver and Harriet Tubman. Others can write prayers for those who lived between the time of Tubman and Martin Luther King. Still others can write prayers for those who suffer today. Hang the timeline on a wall, putting the children's prayers above it.

2) Have youngsters research about a recent natural disaster, such as an earthquake or famine. Ask them to bring in articles, have them report scenes from television news, etc. Post pictures in the classroom. Then the children can study the culture of these people. Discuss the loss of so many people, and the way of life the survivors are enduring now. Invite the children to prepare a brief prayer service.

More about This Saint

Peter Claver (1581-1654), left his homeland of Spain when he was twenty-nine. Influenced by another holy man, Alphonsus Rodriguez, Claver chose to dedicate himself as a Jesuit missioner. He wanted to serve the Africans captured for the booming slave trade to the Americas. Peter worked for forty years in what is now Colombia, despite strong opposition to his work.

A quiet, simple man blessed with great energy, Peter had a deep prayer life. His strong relationship with Jesus enabled him to face the tremendous suffering and injustice he encountered. It is believed that he baptized 300,000 Africans as he carried out his work of mercy. Peter Claver was canonized by Pope Leo XXIII in 1888. His feast day is September 9.

A Story of Saint Zita

Blessed are the meek, for they shall inherit the earth.
—Matthew 5:5

In the beatitude, "Blessed are the meek," Jesus teaches us the importance of being humble and having self-control. Zita, a little-known Italian saint, is an example of the importance God gives to meekness. But who are the meek? Our English word conjures up negative images of a spineless, cowering person. In the Greek language, however, the word for "meek" is *praus*, a very significant ethical word. Aristotle saw meekness as the healthy medium between anger and apathy. *Praus* can also be compared to humility. Humility prepares us to learn because through it we recognize our lack of knowledge.

Our interpretation of this beatitude might be, "O the blessedness of those who are angry at the right times, have self-control because of trust in God's guidance, and who have the humility to realize their own weakness."

The Story

Select ten readers for this story. Have them read their parts silently; encourage them to ask for help with unfamiliar words before reading the story for the class.

Reader One	Zita poured flour into a bowl. She had just come back from early morning Mass, and it was time to make the bread. The kitchen was large and well-stocked, but it was not a happy place.
Reader Two	It served the wealthy family of Pagano de Fatinelli and their servants. Everyone wondered about this maid, Zita. She was kind, considerate, and reliable. Was she up to something?
Reader Three	Zita got up during the night to pray. Often, she gave away her own food to poor and sick people. This bothered the other servants and some family members.
Reader Four	They began treating her harshly. Zita did not protest. She was cheerful and did her duties carefully. Now the other servants became angry with her. They were afraid she made them look careless.
Reader Five	One day, the housekeeper called, "Zita! There's a sick person at the door, asking for you. Don't be all day about it. There is bread to be baked!"

Reader Six	While Zita hurried to the door, the housekeeper declared, "I am going to tell Mr. Fatinelli! She's wasting time again!" The other kitchen maids glanced nervously at each other, for the master had a bad temper.
Reader Seven	As Zita took care of the sick person at the door, she was not aware that all the house servants had come into the kitchen. They were waiting to see what would happen when the angry master found Zita practicing charity. Soon, most of the family had joined them, too. Everyone waited.
Reader Eight	Mr. Fatinelli stormed into the kitchen, the housekeeper following quickly. But they stopped in their tracks. Everyone else turned to see why. At the table where Zita had left her breadmaking, stood majestic angels, mixing, kneading, and shaping the bread dough!
Reader Nine	The kitchen was so quiet, Zita's gentle voice could be heard coming from the doorway. Everyone there realized that Zita was a holy woman. She had become so holy that angels came to do her work!
Reader Ten	No longer would Zita be mistreated. No longer would her service to others be discouraged. This was a fortunate household. How lucky they were to have gentle and meek Zita!

Activities

1) The term "self-control" is not often explained to children. Discuss with them what it means, explaining that Jesus asks us to make good decisions about how we talk and act. Have them silently think of a time when they did not show self-control. Challenge them to look for times during the coming week when they practice self-control. They can share these times in class, if they are comfortable doing so.

2) Ask the children to think of a book or movie they have enjoyed. Each child can name one character who showed humility.

More about This Saint

Saint Zita's last name (1218-1278) is lost to history, since her family was considered unimportant. At age twelve, she began work as a servant to a wealthy merchant. Despite her own lowly status, Zita served the poor and needy who flocked to her door, and she visited hospitals and prisons. She prayed regularly each day, and her whole life was an expression of religious devotion. Her patience with those who mistreated her at work was remarkable. Eventually she was not only accepted but respected. She was assigned to care for the family's children, and later held the position of housekeeper. Pope Pius XII canonized her in 1953, naming her patron of domestic workers. Her feast day is April 27.

A Story of Saint Nicholas

Blessed are those who hunger and thirst for righteousness, for they shall be satisfied.
—Matthew 5:6

Jesus taught by words and example that we must long for and work for justice. Saint Nicholas, a fourth-century bishop, is well known as the generous gift giver we call Santa Claus. It is less well known that he also fought for the rights of the poor and defended those who were wronged, just as Jesus taught.

When Jesus spoke of hunger and thirst, he was speaking to people who often knew real hunger and thirst firsthand. Hot, fierce winds could whirl sand around travelers, causing them to be literally dying for lack of liquid. It was this kind of hunger and thirst that Jesus meant—a sharp, intense, prolonged yearning for good to triumph over evil, justice over injustice. This beatitude can be the most demanding one, for it challenges us to desire goodness above all else. What would we have to fight against, give up, strive for, sweat for, suffer for, if we truly sought goodness?

If the feeling of gnawing, ceaseless hunger was finally eased—what a blessing that would be! We might interpret this beatitude as "O the blessedness of those who long and strive for justice to triumph over injustice, as the starving long for food and the thirsty seek water, for they shall be satisfied."

The Story

To involve your whole class in this story, invite children to imitate your motions. Challenge them to do so dramatically but in silence. Another option would be to have one child who is comfortable with performing stand next to the narrator to do the suggested motions, interpreting the story for the audience. These methods will work best with younger children. The motions can be omitted with older students.

Narrator	The Roman General Ursus was enjoying his dinner (make eating motions). He and two other generals were visiting Bishop Nicholas of Myra. They could see how prayerful he was (fold hands as in prayer), and how seriously he took his duties as bishop. Nicholas was speaking of his concern for those who were hungry when the door burst open (raise hands to face as if startled). A man rushed in, breathless from running (take deep breaths). He cried out, "Good bishop, please pardon my interruption, but three innocent men are about to die because the consul has taken a bribe! We need your help!" (make frantic beckoning motions).

Nicholas sprang to his feet. His gentleness vanished. Now he reminded Ursus of a lion as he bounded for the door. Ursus and the others ran after the bishop and messenger (make motions with arms as if running). They reached the site where an executioner stood above three cowering men. "Stop!" Nicholas bellowed (make "stop" motion, palms outward).

Astonished, Ursus saw the dignified bishop dive at the executioner, knocking him to the ground. "These men are innocent!" he shouted into the executioner's face (make a glaring angry face). Still pinning the executioner to the ground, Nicholas directed the messenger, "Take these men to safety. I will deal with the rest."

The tall bishop got up. Not bothering to brush himself off, he headed swiftly down the street toward the consul's house, while the generals tried to keep up. Nicholas pounded on the door, even trying to break it open (make pounding motions). A very nervous consul rushed to the door babbling, "Ah, Bishop Nicholas! How good of you to come! I was just about to let you in...."

"You enemy of God, how dare you order those men's deaths?" roared Nicholas. The generals watched in astonishment as the bishop berated the consul who was now crying (make crying and pleading motions) and pleading for forgiveness. Finally, Nicholas composed himself, and blessed the consul (make blessing gesture).

Ursus marveled as the bishop walked back to his home, stopping to greet children along the way.

Activities

1) Help children think of a person in our time who works for justice. Write a letter to that person, praising him or her for living this beatitude.

2) Have each student ask someone at home to name a person who works for justice. Have them take notes to share in class.

More about This Saint

Nicholas (c. 280-350) is one of the most beloved saints. Over two thousand churches, hospitals, and monasteries are named for him, and many countries and groups of people claim him as patron. It is known that he was a bishop in what is now Turkey, imprisoned for five years during the Christian persecutions, and that he attended the Council of Nicaea in 325. It is believed that he performed many miracles before and after his death. Stories show his tremendous compassion for the vulnerable, particularly children. But they also show that he went beyond compassion to action, for Nicholas was known for his work for justice. Over the centuries, he became the Christmas gift-bringer because of his generosity and love for children. However, because of his insistence on and struggle for justice, he can be a patron for those who hunger and thirst for righteousness. His feast day is December 6.

A Story of Saint Bathildis

Blessed are the merciful, for they shall obtain mercy.
—Matthew 5:7

What does Jesus mean by "mercy"? The Hebrew word for "mercy" is *chesedh*, translated as the ability to get inside another person's skin, to see with his or her eyes and feel with his or her feelings.

The ultimate example of this mercy is Jesus. Through him, God felt emotions as humans do, saw things through human eyes, felt human pain, and thought with a human mind. We can strive for this fullness of compassion and mercy, and if we do, the beatitude says that we will be treated mercifully, too. Using the Old Testament literary form, we can interpret this beatitude as, "O the blessedness of those who get 'inside' another, to see, think, and feel just as the other person does. They will know that this is what God has done for us in Jesus Christ."

In the seventh century, a little-known saint showed mercy in a big way. Her name was Bathildis.

The Story

Share this story with your class by reading it aloud or by having four readers take turns. If children are reading, practice beforehand.

Reader One	Queen Bathildis sat quietly in her room. Once again everything had changed in an instant. It seemed as if her life was made of chapters, each one vastly different from the other. She had been a happy child in England, where she had been taught to love Jesus. Then one day, she was kidnapped by people greedy for money. She was taken from home and made a slave in France.
Reader Two	How, she wondered, had she ever survived that? But she had. She became a household slave in the palace of King Clovis II. She had worked hard, and by some accounts was also very pretty. In any case, Clovis had noticed her, and another chapter began. Bathildis the slave became Bathildis the queen. Eventually she gave birth to three little princes.
Reader Three	Bathildis roused herself from her chair to gaze out the window. Today one chapter had ended and another chapter had begun, for her husband the king had died. Their oldest son, Clotaire, was crown prince, but he was only five. She was a widow, a mother, an ex-slave, and a Christian. Now she was also queen-regent. She held the power of the throne until little Clotaire could rule.

Reader Four	She must pray for guidance. She must raise her precious sons to become good leaders, strong in their faith. In the meantime she must also be a good leader herself. She must understand fully the people she would rule.
Reader One	She knew with her whole heart what it meant to be a slave. Bathildis shuddered when she thought of the fear and loneliness she had experienced. Now she could free slaves and send them back home! She would also work against the practice of slavery.
Reader Two	She also knew what it meant to be hungry and poor, not to know when there would be another meal. Now she had what she needed, but she vowed to help others who suffered from poverty.
Reader Three	Bathildis knew well what it meant to pray, to want to live a holy life. At times she wanted nothing more. She would start a monastery where others could learn to live for God.
Reader Four	She turned from the window to face her duties. Bathildis was a queen, but she would only be a good one if she knew how it felt to be a frightened slave, a hungry child, a lost soul. A good queen knew the hearts of her people. A good queen was a merciful queen.

Activities

1) Have the children finish the story of Bathildis by illustrating how she fulfilled the vows she made: raising her sons to be merciful, prayerful people; working with enslaved people; helping those who were poor and hungry; having monasteries built for prayer and education.

2) Have the children look in the New Testament (or a children's Bible) for examples of Jesus showing mercy toward others.

More about This Saint

Saint Bathildis' life reads like a fairy tale, but she must have received a remarkable Christian upbringing, for it was a stable force in a life that underwent dramatic changes. Her religion kept her strong and guided her in many situations, decisions, and duties. In addition to her work to end slavery and poverty (she sold royal jewels to raise money) and her opposition to oppressive taxes, Bathildis endowed monasteries and founded an abbey at Chelles. After her sons had grown, the queen left her public life behind to enter the convent at the abbey she had begun. She lived there for fifteen years in great simplicity until her death in 680. Her feast day is January 30.

A Story of Saint Joseph of Cupertino

Blessed are the pure in heart, for they shall see God.
—Matthew 5:8

As we continue our study of the beatitudes in the lives of saints, we encounter a particularly charming saint, Joseph of Cupertino. He was so "pure of heart" that he was able to experience God as few ever have before or after him. The Greek word for pure is *katharos*, which means unmixed or unadulterated. What appears to be simple advice from Jesus is actually a difficult task: how often do we choose to do something from purely unselfish (unmixed) motives?

Even our most basic actions, such as sending a friend a card, may stem from obligation or hopes of recompense. This beatitude challenges us to do an exacting self-examination. What are our motives when we pray, help others, or reach out to those we teach?

We can interpret this beatitude as "O the blessedness of those whose motives are absolutely clean, unmixed with worldly concerns, for someday they will see God."

The Story

Choose two readers for the main parts of the story, and encourage the other children to join in the chorus.

Reader One	Joseph was a failure. He had failed at being a shoemaker and a monk. He had not even been a very successful child! Everyone in his village called him clumsy and foolish. Even as an adult, he broke dishes, spilled water, and tripped over things. He was so clumsy, even the monks asked him to leave.
All	But Joseph was pure in heart!
Reader Two	The only place poor Joseph seemed to fit in was a stable where he was put in charge of a donkey. "Well," Joseph decided, "if I am going to be a stable boy, I will do the best I can." He called himself "Little Donkey" because no one expected much from him.
All	But Joseph was pure in heart!
Reader One	Joseph worked hard at his simple job. He was cheerful, even when others made fun of him. As he worked, he prayed. The more Joseph prayed, the happier he felt. When his work with the donkey was finished, he would wander off into the meadows where he prayed to God and talked with the meadow

animals. The love he felt from God and the love he felt for God's creatures filled him with great joy. Stories tell that he became so happy that one day his happiness lifted him off the ground! Joseph could actually fly!

All	Joseph was pure of heart!
Reader Two	Of course people soon heard about the flying. They flocked to see Joseph. They were astonished to see him lifted up, and they were deeply moved by his joy. It was easy and wonderful to see the purity of Joseph's love for God. People began bringing sick people to Joseph. He would touch them, and sometimes, they were healed!
All	Joseph was pure of heart!
Reader One	Seeing how much Joseph loved God, the monks invited him to become a priest. Even though he had trouble with his studies, he was eventually ordained. He continued his simple tasks, spending much time in prayer. Though the monks wanted a quiet life, crowds would come to see Joseph. It was said that people saw him lifted in the air seventy times!
All	Joseph was certainly pure of heart!
Reader Two	When Joseph was sixty years old, he became ill. "Little Donkey" had lived his life with a "pureness of heart" that helped him experience God in extraordinary ways. And he died with a smile on his face!

Activities

1) Read the picture book *The Little Friar Who Flew*, by Patricia Lee Gauch, illustrated by Tomie de Paola, Putnam, 1980. This may be available in public libraries.

2) Discuss with the children what it means to have no motive but goodness. List on the board several common experiences, such as helping a friend with homework, telling a joke, talking about people behind their backs, or giving a gift. Talk about different motives people might have in each circumstance. Help the children see how difficult it is to have pure motives. Suggest that for a week, they do a examination of their motives each day.

More about This Saint

Joseph Desa, born in Cupertino, Italy, in 1602, lived with the pure motive of loving God. After an impoverished childhood, and failing as an apprentice shoemaker, he applied for admission with the Franciscans and Capuchins, but both dismissed him for being inept and unreliable. Through the help of an uncle, he was accepted by the Franciscans as a servant. It was there that his simple yet extraordinary spirituality flourished. His life was irrevocably changed by it, but his simplicity and intent never wavered. He died on September 18, 1663, was canonized a saint in 1767, and later, was named patron of aviators—of course! His feast day is September 18.

A Story of Saint Catherine of Siena

Blessed are the peacemakers, for they shall be called children of God.
—Matthew 5:9

In his wisdom, Jesus tells us with this beatitude to work for peace. Peacemaking ranges from small acts of kindness to protesting an injustice. It takes on much greater proportions in the international setting, and each era has its prominent peacemakers, such as Francis of Assisi, Abraham Lincoln, Jane Addams, and Jimmy Carter. In the fourteenth century, a mystic, Catherine of Siena, worked for peace on several levels, emerging as one of the most vital peacemakers of her time.

A peacemaker does not avoid conflicts to maintain peace, but deals with difficulties. Sometimes the only way to peace is through the conflict. When Jesus spoke of a peacemaker, he may have been referring to someone who establishes "right relationships" between people, which Jewish rabbis held as the highest task a person could perform.

In the Hebrew language, a phrase, rather than one word, is used to describe a person, the most common phrase being "son of," along with a noun. The English term peacemaker would be "son of peace" in Hebrew. Jesus' words "sons of God" (or children of God) can be translated to mean "O the blessings of those who bring about right relationships between people, for they are doing Godlike work."

The Story

Explain that Catherine was a very unusual woman for her time, as most women had little power outside of their homes. Also, tell children that Catherine's work and holiness attracted many followers. Choose three readers to play the parts of three fictional monks who worked with Catherine. Help the other children join in on the chorus.

Brother Thaddeus	I am a monk living in the city of Siena; I'm one of the followers of the wise and learned Catherine. She is remarkable in her holiness as well as her wisdom, so she has many followers. With the help of some other followers, I would like to tell you about what she does. We are certain that someday, Catherine will be a great saint. We are honored to assist her in her work.
All	Catherine was strong and good, and Jesus made her a peacemaker.
Brother Callistus	Like most women of our time Catherine cannot read or write, so she dictates letters to us. These letters are sent to lords and other nobles who are fighting amongst themselves and have asked for her help in settling their conflicts.

	Sometimes Catherine goes to talk with people from both sides. Little by little, she helps them see ways to compromise, to work things out. We are always astonished at what she can accomplish.
All	Catherine was strong and good, and Jesus made her a peacemaker.
Brother Caedmon	We have never been as astonished as we were a few months ago when Catherine asked us to write a letter to the pope! And this was no ordinary letter, asking for his blessing. Oh no! Catherine was giving him advice in the form of a gift. You see, the popes have always lived in Rome. We consider it a holy city. But lately, there has been much fighting in Rome, and the pope fled to a place in France called Avignon. Catherine believes that it is God's will that the pope go back to Rome, so she found a clever way of telling him so. She sent him candied orange peel as a Christmas gift, along with a letter that says, "The taste of this gift is at first bitter, then sweet. That is how it is when you do God's will."
All	Catherine was strong and good, and Jesus made her a peacemaker.
Brother Thaddeus	Will Catherine be successful with the pope? Perhaps. She is guided by Jesus, and is powerful because of her devotion to Christ. So why were we so surprised that she should write to the pope? Jesus has been preparing her for this for a long time. All her life, actually. She is the youngest child—the twenty-fifth!—of Giacomo and Lapa Benincasa, prosperous wool-dyers. As a child she was friendly and cheerful, but liked to spend time alone. When she was only six years old, she had a vision. She saw Jesus with the saints Peter, Paul, and John. She decided then and there that she belonged to Jesus and that she would spend her life serving him.
All	Catherine was strong and good, and Jesus made her a peacemaker.
Brother Callistus	Catherine's parents wanted her to marry a wealthy man, but she refused. She said she wanted to be the bride of Christ. Fearful that they would pressure her more, she cut off her long hair! What a shock that was for her parents! At first they were angry, but then her father had a vision of a dove above Catherine's head as she prayed. He took this as a sign that Catherine should follow a religious life. She joined the Third Order of Dominicans, a group of women who lived at home and wore a habit. For three years she lived mostly in her room, praying and having many visions. Then, she was ready to serve Jesus in the world.
All	Catherine was strong and good, and Jesus made her a peacemaker.
Brother Caedmon	Catherine has many followers—monks like myself, laywomen and men, and priests. She has such a spiritual way about her! I can only say that she is the holiest person I have ever known. It has been a privilege to help her in her work as peacemaker. We aid the poor, visit prisoners, and serve the sick and dying. As to the pope, Catherine will continue writing to him, I am sure! I keep my writing utensils ready and a traveling bag nearby. I will not be surprised if she decides to go to France, to meet with the pope himself. She greatly desires peace in the Church.

Activities

1) Have the children make a mural of scenes from Catherine's life: her visions as a child, cutting her hair, her father seeing the dove over her head, helping people to work out conflicts, talking to the pope. Give the children several pieces of paper and markers, crayons, and watercolors. On each piece, they can draw and paint a scene. On a large wall, hang these artworks together to form a mural.

2) Make a peace quilt out of paper to hang on the wall. Give each youngster a square of white paper. Each one can draw a dove for peace and write the name of someone they think of as a peacemaker. Encourage the artists to use much color and to create designs around the doves and names. Tape the squares to a wall in a quilt-like pattern.

More about This Saint

Catherine of Siena (1347-1380), is considered one of the greatest saints of a tumultuous era. The "Black Death" plague raged, there was continuous fighting among European cities, and the pope fled from Italy to France, thus leaving the Church in the hands of corrupt administrators. After a remarkable period of solitude, visions, and other miraculous signs while she was in her late teens, Catherine emerged into public life. First she did works of charity, then became involved in peacemaking on a local scale, then negotiations in religious politics. She wrote, by dictation, hundreds of letters, counseling public figures on the performance of their duties. Her book, *The Dialogue*, has been ranked with the writings of Dante. She did travel to France to speak with the pope. Respectfully but uncompromisingly, she advised and made changes. She continued to work for unity during the Great Western Schism, when the conflict became so great that two popes were elected. The stress of this work caused her to suffer two strokes. She died at age thirty-three. She is remembered as a person who shaped the Church of her time, a mystic, and peacemaker. In 1970, the pope named Catherine a Doctor of the Church along with Saint Teresa of Avila, the first two women to be honored this way. Her feast day is April 29.

A Story of
Saint Paul Miki and Companions

Blessed are they who are persecuted for the sake of righteousness
for theirs is the kingdom of heaven.
—Matthew 5:10

This beatitude needs little interpretation, for Christ makes it very clear that those who stand for what is right and, in the case of martyrs, even die for what is right, will reap the benefits in heaven. But martyrs are also witnesses of how to live. Their stories give us encouragement and their prayers can sustain us when we take a stand for Christ. Saint Paul Miki and his companions are ideal examples of this.

The Story

The story of Paul Miki is told by Japanese Christians two hundred years after his death. You can present this as a simple play. Choose readers for the parts of the Narrator, Father Petitjean, the Leader (a female who will have the longest part), and Reader One and Reader Two, who accompany the Leader. The rest of the class will be the group of Christians who are also with the Leader. Any actions needed will be clearly stated in the text.

Narrator	Father Bernard Petitjean looked up from his work to see a small group of people approaching his house. For five years the French priest had worked in Japan, trying to bring the news of Jesus to the people, but with little result. It was only in these past few years, the 1860s, that missioners were allowed into the country. However, many Japanese people seemed afraid to approach them. Curious and hoping for a change, Father Petitjean went to the door, greeted his visitors, and invited them in. They seemed nervous. Then one woman began speaking, but it seemed as if it took all her courage to do so.
The Leader	Father, we are Christians. In secret, we say the prayers you say, celebrate the same feast days, and baptize our children. We were taught all this by our parents, and they by their parents before them.

Father Petitjean	But there hasn't been a Christian missioner here for two hundred years! Your families have kept the faith alive that long? Are there others besides you?
The Leader	Oh yes. Many, many more. Hundreds. Perhaps thousands.
Father Petitjean	Thousands of secret Christians?
The Leader	Yes. It began with the arrival of Francis Xavier in 1591. Within a few decades, there were many Christians. The ruler then was Hideyoshi, who became worried that they might take over. He watched them suspiciously.
Reader One	Among them was Father Paul Miki who came from a wealthy Japanese family. When Hideyoshi decided to crush Christianity, Paul Miki was one of the first arrested. On December 8, 1596, twenty-six men from Maiko were condemned.
Reader Two	Three were Japanese Jesuit priests, one of them Paul, six were Spanish Franciscan priests, and seventeen were Japanese laymen. Some of these were carpenters, doctors, and teachers—and boys. A child named Louis was ten, Anthony was thirteen, Thomas was sixteen, and Gabriel, nineteen.
The Leader	They were forced to walk more than three hundred miles from Maiko to Nagasaki, through snow and ice. Along the way, they preached to many people who gathered to see them march. They sang psalms joyfully, and prayed the rosary, too. They reached Nagasaki on February fifth, where twenty-six crosses awaited them. They were to die as their savior Jesus did.
Reader One	As Paul Miki hung on his cross, he forgave his persecutors, as Jesus did before him.
Reader Two	After these brave men died, there were more deaths, about three thousand known martyrs. The government leaders thought the Christian Church had been destroyed. No missioners were allowed in until now. But the Church did survive "underground," for more than two hundred years.
Father Petitjean	More than two hundred years! And you say there are thousands of Christians! Perhaps the time has come to consider building a memorial to these martyrs, who gave their lives so you could be Christian today!
Narrator	All the people nodded, for yes, the time had come.

Activities

1) Here is a word search with names of martyrs. To accommodate young readers, the words go only across and down. There are no diagonal or backward words. The names to find are listed below. If the martyr has two names, both are used but there is no space between them.

Names to look for: Paul Miki; Valentine; Felicity; Thomas More; James; Philip; Peter; Lucy; Oscar Romero, Stephen, Edith Stein, Maximilian Kolbe.

```
M A X I M I L I A N K O L B E
J P P J A J U M M R K S B T D
L C H M R T C K S J S C C H I
S P I K K D Y M M P M A E O T
F E L I C I T Y D A V R M M H
A T I A P N P L E U C R L A S
J E P W E L E M H L T O K S T
A R S G S C J S L M C M J M E
M K S V A L E N T I N E C O I
E M O D M L S P T K V R E R N
S T E P H E N Q G I A O Z E X
```

2) Discuss with your students what it would have been like to belong to the generation of "underground" Christians in Japan. Have them imagine themselves and their families in that situation. Ask: how do you think your family would practice its beliefs? Who in your home would do the teaching and baptizing? What do you think you would do to help teach others in your home? Do you think religion was more important or less important to those children than it is to you? Why?

More about This Saint

Paul Miki (c. 1564-1597) was born to a wealthy family and educated by Jesuits missioners in Japan. He joined the order in 1580, and became an excellent preacher. As Christianity spread, the government began a period of persecution. Twenty-five companions, from age ten to sixty-four, died with Father Paul. They were the first of thousands of martyrs in the Japanese Christian Church. A cathedral was built at the site of the deaths of Miki and the others. Their feast day is February 6.

Because of these crucifixions, the cross became a particularly important symbol for Japanese Christians. It is a terrible irony that when an American pilot flew over Nagasaki on August 9, 1945, he used the steeple of the Urakami Cathedral as his target in dropping the atomic bomb. Among the seventy-nine thousand people immediately killed were ten thousand Catholics.

PART TWO

Exploring the Wisdom of Vatican II Teachings

Stories of Neighbors in the Modern World

Introduction

The Catholic Church has a checkered past in its role in teaching and practicing justice. Jewish people were massacred by Christian crusaders; cultures were lost when missionaries and the explorers who accompanied them brought Western civilization to other lands. On the other hand, many Catholics died trying to save their Jewish brothers and sisters during World War II, others fought against the kidnapping and enslavement of Africans to the Americas, monks risked their lives to minister to the dying during deadly plagues, and religious leaders like Oscar Romero have spoken and acted on behalf of the poor. Drastic changes in the world's order brought about by wars, scientific advancements, shifts in political power, etc., have always challenged those who seek to live the gospel. There have been triumphs and failures over the centuries.

In the recent past, the twentieth century was ushered in with problems brought about by the Industrial Revolution. It also brought bishops working for social reforms, religious orders opening schools and hospitals, and Pope Leo XIII's encyclical, *Rerum Novarum*. Written in 1891, this encyclical stated the individual's right to private property and the worker's right to form associations and to receive a just wage. It criticized exploitation, and warned against organizations hostile to both state and religion. In short, Leo XIII laid the groundwork for the Church's dialogue with the modern world.

The first half of the twentieth century saw this work challenged by increasing changes in technology and industry, and by World Wars I and II. However, numerous theologians were laboring to bring the Church back to its ancient roots of faith while reflecting on the Church's mission within the world's forum.

In mid-century, into the papacy stepped John XXIII. His work had given him varied experiences in Bulgaria, Turkey, France, and Italy, with Catholics living in Muslim and Orthodox countries, and with Catholics of Latin, Greek, and Syrian backgrounds. He was well aware of the work and experience of the theologians. All this left him determined to find new ways for the Church to take its place in the modern world. Pope John summoned an ecumenical council, Vatican II. More than 2500 bishops attended. They came from Australia, Central, South, and North Americas, Asia, Africa, and Europe. The council lasted for more than three years and brought major changes for the years to come.

Among the many studies and writings that resulted, one of the most significant was *Gaudium et Spes*, or *The Pastoral Constitution on the Church in the Modern World*. Cardinal Suenens of Belgium proposed the writing of this document out of concern for the poor of the world. He urged the council to create a practical theology regarding the responsibilities of rich nations towards poor nations. He wanted the Church to be prepared to answer the question, "Church of Christ, what do you have to say for yourself?"

A simple yet profound answer to this question may be found in the preface: "The joys and hopes, the griefs and the anxieties of ...this age, especially those who are poor and in any way afflicted, these too are the joys and hopes, the griefs and anxieties of the followers of Christ."

The underlying theme of *The Church in the Modern World* is that the Church is the servant of the human family. As teachers and parents, we must prepare our children to meet the world as Christians. They must learn to see, feel, and act in terms of the joys, hopes, griefs, and anxieties of their brothers and sisters around the globe. The following stories are meant to begin that process.

Using Part Two

Sections from the text of *The Church in the Modern World* set the scene for the following modern-day stories. The text is listed for your reflection. Before going on to the story, do the activities in "Doing the Groundwork," listed below. As children may not have had much exposure to world geography, these activities will help them have a better sense about where the stories take place, and what these places are like.

The stories in each chapter are either fiction based on real circumstances or stories about real children. All are written to help your students better identify with their peers throughout the world, an essential to living justly. There is a follow-up activity, "Our World Booklets," to be done after each story is read. Instructions are given below. Each chapter also contains suggestions for discussion.

Activities

Doing the Groundwork

A) Bring to your religion class books about the country or countries in the story. Public libraries have wonderful nonfiction books for children about a variety of countries, filled with beautiful photos and facts. Also, ask a children's reference librarian if there are any fiction books set in these countries that are suitable for the age group you work with. Display all the books in a place where children can easily see and reach them.

B) Pin up a piece of poster board. In large letters print the name of the country you will study. Have the children use the nonfiction books to find information about the country. They can call out the information and you write it on the posterboard. Children can also draw the country's flag, or something else significant for this country. If any children are interested in reading fiction books set in this country, allow them to take those books home (make sure they understand they are responsible for returning the books to you). Later they can contribute what they learned to the poster or to class discussions.

C) Display a world map while you work with Part Two. Each time you read a story, locate on the map the country or countries mentioned in it. Place a marker on the country, leaving the markers in place as you explore more countries.

Our World Booklets

A separate but related project is "Our World" booklets the children can make. The children make books by stapling pieces of drawing paper together. They divide each page in half, either horizontally or vertically. On each page they compare certain aspects in their own lives and that of the story character. These can be school, home, family, church, toys, transportation, food, etc. Encourage them to look for similarities and differences. The comparisons can be written, drawn, or both. Give the children colorful paper to create covers for their finished books. A booklet could be made for each story so the children will have a small library of cultural information.

Anastazja Learns How to Be a Neighbor

A Story from Albania

This story will help children understand Chapter 11, part 27 from *The Church in the Modern World* (paraphrased here):

In our time, a special obligation binds us to make ourselves the neighbors of every person without exception, actively helping others when they cross our path. These persons may be elderly persons who are without a family, workers from another country who are looked down on here, refugees, homeless children, or hungry persons. Any of these people may disturb our conscience and help us hear the Lord who said, "As long as you did this for the least of my brethren, you did it for me" (Matthew 25:40).

Doing the Groundwork

Before reading the story, bring in books on Albania, start the poster, and locate on the map the countries mentioned in the story, as explained on page 29.

The Story

The following story can be read in parts. You will need four readers in addition to yourself. The parts are: Teacher, Mama, Jorgi, and Krista and Anastazja. The latter two have the most significant reading parts.

Teacher	This story is set in eastern Europe, mainly Albania, a very mountainous country about the size of the state of Maryland. By European standards, it is an extremely poor country. Roads are in disrepair, and most families cannot afford a car, so people walk and take trains. Most homes have electricity but no running water or telephones. The majority of people have only two sets of clothing. There are three main religious groups, the largest being Islam, then Orthodox, and last, Roman Catholicism. The following story takes place in the recent past when Serbian soldiers forced people in nearby Kosovo to flee their country and seek refuge in Albania.
Krista	My name is Krista, and I am nine years old. Until the war began, I lived in Kosovo with my parents, four brothers, and my grandmother. When Serbian soldiers entered our town, they burst into our house with guns in their hands. They told us that we had to leave. I was home with my mother, grandmother, and younger brother. We were not allowed to pack. I could not even bring my

doll, which I've had since I was three years old. We couldn't wait for the rest of the family to come home—not with those soldiers' guns pointed at us. My mother carried my little brother. Grandmother and I held hands, and we walked away from our home.

Anastazja	My name is Anastazja, and I am ten years old. I live in Albania in a small house with my parents, two younger brothers, and a baby sister. Because I am the oldest, Mama, my *nene*, wakes me when the rooster crows, so I can get the day's water before I go to school. I take our donkey to the spring to carry the pails, but it is still a long walk. On laundry days, I have to bring extra pails. There are always diapers to wash! I try not to slosh water on my shoes, for they are my only pair.
	One morning as I brought in the water, my parents were listening to the radio as usual. As I ate my bread and honey, I heard about the war in nearby Kosovo. Thousands of people were being forced to leave their homes! Mama was giving the baby, Liria, a sip of *qumesht* or milk.
Mama	Where will they go? How will they eat? What will happen when it gets cold?
Anastazja	My father finished his coffee and shook his head at the sad news. He then kissed each of us, and headed off to his factory job.
Mama	We are blessed that your father still has a job. So many people don't.
Anastazja	Then Mama kissed me and wished me a good day at school. But I knew she was thinking about the people who had to leave their homes. My brother Jorgi and I set off on the four-mile walk to school. "Someday, Jorgi," I said, "I want to go to the university!"
Jorgi	Maybe there you won't have to share a desk.
Anastazja	I laughed. "You keep growing, Jorgi, and you will only have to share with one other person. It's only the smallest students who sit three to a desk. Come on, let's race!"
Krista	Thousands of people were forced to leave their homes in Kosovo. My grandmother, mother, brother, and I arrived at the border with hundreds of others. We were all hoping to get into Albania. Many, many were children. I saw fear and unhappiness everywhere. Here, if we were lucky, we would be able to sleep. I felt frightened. But it was a different kind of fear than when the soldiers came into our house. And I was so hungry, I felt dizzy. Grandmother held my little brother, who was crying with hunger. We found a space in a tent, then my mother walked around, asking for news about the rest of my family. When mother returned, she had a loaf of bread and a blanket. She said nothing about my father and brothers. After our meal we huddled close together and tried to go to sleep in the chilly tent. We did not know what the next day would bring.
Anastazja	When Jorgi and I came home from school, our father was home. He was wearing his old sweater with the patched elbows. Father said to Mama, "We don't

have much to spare." Mama shrugged her shoulders. "No, but what is asked of us as Christians? These people have nothing, and they are our neighbors," she said. My father nodded, saying, "I'll watch the young ones. You and Anastazja go." So I looked to Mama who was packing clothing and food.

| Mama | Put your scarf on, Anastazja. We are going to the refugee camp. |

| Krista | We were allowed into a refugee camp now. It was a whole city of tents! Relief workers were hurrying about, bringing in supplies of food, water, clothing, and medicine. Children were running about everywhere, and schools were set up in certain tents. Relief workers had organized art projects and soccer teams, too. My little brother clung to my mother, but I explored. The camp was crowded and noisy, and it was easy to feel lost. |

| Teacher | Anastazja's mother encouraged her friends to join her in visiting the refugee camps. There they met women and children like themselves. The difference was that the refugees now had nothing, not even a place to take a bath. The Albanian women invited many of the Kosovar women and children to their homes. There, the Albanians offered baths, hot tea, conversation, and a chance to feel normal again. That is how Anastazja and Krista became friends. |

| Krista | Anastazja's home was small, but we felt very welcome. Her mother served us soup out of a pot she had made from a coffee can. She is a clever person, my mother says. Baby Liria slept nearby, and our little brothers played outside. It felt so good, as if none of the bad things had ever happened! Anastazja asked me to come to her bedroom, which she shared with her brothers. It was a cold room, so she lent me the extra sweater her mother had knitted. Pretty soon we were laughing together. |

| Anastazja | My mother invited Krista and her family to our house often. Our mothers became friends, and so did Krista and I. In my bedroom, I told her jokes, and she knew such great ghost stories that chills ran down my spine! We talked about school, too. One day, Krista told me about the day the soldiers came to her house. Looking at my two dolls, she said she even had to leave her doll behind. I felt badly for her, so I planned a picnic. Mama gave us oranges and tea, and we went outside. Holding up my cup of tea, I suggested, "Let's pretend this is a beautiful castle, and we are rich women who always have lots of good things to eat!" Krista said, in an exaggerated voice, "Oh, darling, that is a simply beautiful gown you are wearing!" We both looked at my old dress and began to giggle. We laughed all afternoon, and everything seemed all right. |

| Teacher | When the war ended, many Kosovars returned home. The roads into Kosovo were crowded with trucks and tractors. They were pulling wagons filled with weary but hopeful people like Krista and her family. Many families found their homes, schools, and stores burned, roofless, or damaged in other ways. The United Nations and relief organizations had trucks sent in with much-needed supplies. Families began to reunite. They began the process of rebuilding their lives. |

Anastazja   Krista's mother received news that the rest of the family was safe. Soon after, Krista and her family returned home. Many other refugees have to remain here, and my mother invites them over. But I know she misses Krista's mother. I miss Krista, too. But sometimes at night when I am in bed, I hear my little brothers sleeping. I think of how glad Krista must be to be back with all her brothers. And I look at my one doll, and am glad that the other one is with Krista in Kosovo.

Activities

Our World Booklets

Help the children begin their booklets as described on page 29.

Discussion Starters

- Discuss with your children what the word "neighbor" means. Then read aloud Luke 10:29–37, the parable of the Good Samaritan, in which Jesus defines what a neighbor is.
- Using this definition, ask:
  - How did Anastazja's family act as neighbors?
  - Who has treated you as a neighbor?
  - How can we be good neighbors?
  - Is there someone you find very hard to treat as a neighbor? What can you do to make sure you treat them as Jesus would?

Furaha's Lesson

A Story from Tanzania

This story helps children understand Chapter 2, part 31 in *The Church in the Modern World* (paraphrased here):

We must make sure that all young people, from every part of society, are well-educated. Through education, we will produce the kind of women and men so urgently needed today, people who are not only highly cultured but are generous in spirit as well.

Doing the Groundwork

Before reading the story, bring in books on Tanzania, begin the poster, and locate Tanzania on the map, as explained on page 29.

The Story

This story is fictional but based on information from the newsletter *Jump* (Junior Mission Partners, formerly *Kids Care News*) and the video, *The Field Afar: Msamge, Tanzania*, both available through Maryknoll. (See Part Four for more information).

To read this story, you will need readers for these parts: Teacher, Grandmother, Furaha, Girl, and Readers 1, 2, 3, 4, and 5.

Teacher

This story takes place in Tanzania, the largest country in Eastern Africa. It is just south of the equator. Most of the people are farmers. The houses in small villages are made from bamboo, thatch, and tin. The people cook over open fires, and most homes have no electricity or running water. Some children walk as far as four miles every day to get water.

Tanzania is home to many different groups of people, or tribes. This could cause fighting. However, Tanzanians work for *ujaama*, or cooperation, so there is great peace among the many peoples. They also believe education is important, and there are schools for all children through seventh grade. There are not enough high schools for everyone, however.

In our story, we meet Furaha, who wants to attend high school. In order for her to do this, her parents will have to find extra jobs or sell something very valuable, like a farm animal.

Reader One	Furaha sat on the ground, looking up at the moon above the tin-roofed houses of her village. She listened to the night breezes. Her mother was settling the younger children to sleep. Grandmother was singing softly. These were sweet sounds that Furaha would miss. Her name means "happiness" but tonight she was sad and scared. In the morning, she would leave her village to go to a boarding school for girls, run by a missioner sister. When Furaha had finished seventh grade, she dreamed of going to high school. But there were not many such schools, and they were far away. Probably she would do what most of the others girls in her village did: marry around the age of sixteen or seventeen. Then her parents learned of this new school and wanted her to go. Tomorrow she would leave for school, and she was scared. Grandmother came out of the tiny house to sit by Furaha.
Grandmother	I had your father by the time I was your age. But you, Furaha, will go to school!
Furaha	(nervous, tracing the pattern on her *rubeka* [her dress] with her fingers) I want to go, but I'm frightened, Grandmother!
Grandmother	Of course, I would be too. All things are hard at the beginning. Just try to remember how much your parents have given up so you can go to school. What you learn at school will help our family and others in the village. And those you teach will teach others. Always remember: whatever is good, continues on.
Furaha	(smiling) Grandmothers are always telling grandchildren wise sayings.
Grandmother	Then here is another one. Don't give up this opportunity. Don't let it be said that I pointed out the moon to you and all you saw was my finger.
Reader One	With that, Grandmother went back into the little house. Furaha stood looking up at the moon.
Reader Two	The next morning, Furaha said her goodbyes and left her home and family behind. Carrying her belongings on her head, Furaha walked over dusty roads, past fruit trees and the sacred baobab trees. She went on through grasslands and villages. She saw young mothers bringing home the day's supply of water. Gourds filled with water were balanced on their heads, and babies wrapped snugly onto their backs. It was not long before Furaha came to her new school.
Reader Three	Furaha pulled on the white blouse and red sweater and skirt that were now her uniform. It was early morning. As she stood in line with the other girls, she wondered what her family was doing right now. All the girls were singing as they ran off to their first classes of the day. It seemed as if they were always singing. Furaha enjoyed music, but the classes of math, languages, science, history, sewing, and farming were difficult. What if she did not do well? Her parents had worked very hard so she could go to school! She wished she could talk with Grandmother.

Reader Four	In her class, Furaha asked why so many village people were at the school well each morning.
Teacher	When we began the school, we dug a well for our water. Then we saw how our well could help those in the nearby village. Their well was much further away than ours, so we offered them the use of it.
Reader Four	Furaha thought about this now as she walked under the blazing sun to the well, swinging a green bucket. At this time of day there was only one villager there, a girl about Furaha's age. She had a huge, dried gourd which she was filling with water. Furaha smiled shyly at her. The girl smiled back, but her eyes were filled with a kind of envy.
Girl	I can tell by your clothes that you go to the school. I wish I could. You're very lucky.
Furaha	The sister who runs the school is trying to raise more money so more girls can come. Maybe you'll get to come.
Girl	Perhaps...I would like that. Well, study hard.
Reader Four	The girl turned to walk back to her village. As Furaha filled her bucket with water, she thought of Grandmother's words about teaching others what she had learned.
Reader Five	A year passed and Furaha forgot about being shy at school. She sang with delight, laughed with friends, danced with gusto, answered in classes, and studied hard. She did not forget about the girl at the well who could not go to school.
	Now it was time for vacation. As Furaha walked back to her village, she planned what she would teach others at home while she was there. Her little sister could begin to sew. Perhaps someday, the two sisters could sell clothing they made themselves! Furaha had learned new farming methods that her father would be glad to try. Her mother wanted to learn new ways to cook healthy foods. She could teach her brothers and sister about geography and science. And Grandmother? She hoped they would sit under the moon together and sing all the new songs Furaha had learned.

Activities

Our World Booklets

Help the students begin their second booklet, this one about Tanzania.

Discussion Starters

For younger children

- Discuss what it means to be generous in spirit.

- What do your children teach others? What skills do they have to share?

- Read Grandmother's proverbs and discuss what they mean. Suggest the children ask family members for other proverbs.

For older children

- Challenge them to define "highly cultured and "generous in spirit." Do they see themselves in these terms?

- The literacy rate in Tanzania is 68%, one of the highest in Africa. Have children research the literacy rate in other countries.

- Life expectancy for Tanzanians is 44 years for men, 48 years for women. Have children compare this to the United States and other countries. Discuss why there are such great differences.

- Furaha's family's income would be about $200-300, and tuition could be as high as $135. The cost of tuition, then, would be 45% to 67% of the family's income. In the United States public high school is free. Discuss with the children how their families would pay for school if it cost more than half of their families' income.

Ramir's Christmas Message

A Story from the Philippines

This story will help children understand Part 1, Number 11 from *The Church in the Modern World* (paraphrased here):

As people of God, we believe we are led by the Holy Spirit who fills the whole world. Driven by this faith, we look for signs of God's presence and purpose in the world. We look at our needs and desires to see what we have in common with the rest of God's people. For faith casts a new light on everything. It tells us what greatness God wants for his people and guides our minds toward solutions that will help bring this about.

Doing the Groundwork

Before reading the story, bring in books on the Philippines, start the poster, and locate the Philippine Islands on the map.

The Story

Some of the factual information for this fictional story was generously supplied by Maryknoll Sister Jeanne Houlihan, in *Kids Care News* (No. 1, Vol. 2). This newsletter is now known as *Jump* (Junior Mission Partners).

You can use eight readers for this story: Readers 1 and 2, Nali, Ramir, Carmel, Father, Luis, and Teacher.

Reader One	Ramir walked down the dusty road, shivering in his school uniform. It must be down to 65 degrees! A few steps ahead of him, his younger brother Benedict and their sisters Carmel and Nali were loudly singing Christmas songs. Six-year-old Nali turned to walk backwards.
Nali	(to Ramir) How many days until we start going to the Misa de Gallo, the Mass of the Rooster?
Reader Two	Ramir groaned a little. Nali was talking about the nine days before Christmas when their family attended Mass each day at 4:00 in the morning.
Ramir	In only three more days.
Nali	I get to go this year, too! But will I wake up in time?
Carmel	(laughing) Don't worry! The church bells won't let you sleep! But we'd better finish our instruments tonight!

Reader One	The three younger children ran ahead, talking about the musical instruments they were making out of coconut shells, empty cans, oil canisters, bamboo sticks, and anything else they could find. They would go out with other neighborhood children singing Christmas carols for others in their town, and playing their instruments.
Reader Two	Ramir had done this for as many years as he could remember, but somehow, this year his heart wasn't in it. Instead, he thought about the pictures he had seen of the great city of Manila, the capital of his country. Today his teacher had shown the class how some of the richest people and some of the poorest people lived in the same city. He remembered the pictures of the poor families living in rows of shacks made of scraps of wood and metal. He thought of children who lived and worked on the city streets. Heading back to his own small home, Ramir did not feel much like celebrating.
Reader One	It was the first of the nine days before Christmas. Ramir yawned. Getting up at 4 a.m. left him feeling sleepy early this evening. All around him, though, his family members were full of energy. Carmel and Lola, their grandmother, had made a Christmas tree out of a palm branch. Benedict decorated it with tiny paper ornaments. His aunt and mother were making food for the Christmas meal. Ramir's mother saved money all year to be able to provide this feast.
Reader Two	Ramir's father was working on the *parol*, the star lantern. The younger children, Nali, Luis, and tiny Mariliza were excitedly trying to help. Ramir looked up at their statue of the Virgin Mary. She seemed to look upon all this festivity with approval.
Father	(laughing) Ramir, I seem to need even more help than I already have!
Reader One	Luis was twirling one of the bamboo sticks. Nali was stepping on the tassels and touching the Japanese paper. Mariliza had glue across her nose. Ramir laughed, too. Then he took the sticks his father had made into a star shape and carefully glued the colorful paper onto them. Luis watched him closely.
Luis	Why do we make this lantern? Where do we hang it? Other people make them too, right?
Father	Everyone makes a *parol*, Luis. It's an important Filipino custom. All over our country, there are small ones, huge ones, fancy and simple ones, but they all do the same thing—light the way for Mary and Joseph traveling to Bethlehem.
Luis	How?
Father	(holding up the star) Now that we've finished, we'll put a light inside it and hang it up outside.
Nali	And Mary and Joseph will see the light and know where to go!
Reader Two	"Pretty!" little Mariliza said. Her dark eyes were shining. She truly believed that Mary and Joseph would pass by their home. Ramir envied her.

Reader One	Ramir sighed as he walked home next day, after the early Mass. Everyone else seemed happy. Nali was even skipping.
Father	You don't seem to be in the spirit, Ramir.
Ramir	(unhappily) Does Christmas matter? We celebrate God becoming human, but what good did it do? Some people are very wealthy people while others starve! Some children sleep on the streets! There is war, and many other kinds of violence. And sickness, too!
Father	Ramir, I am proud of you for being so concerned for others. But God's plan for us is not hunger, war, or sickness. We have faith that God can bring good even out of the bad things caused by greedy people. We look for those signs. And we must look and work for ways to help bring God's plan about. God is with us as we work for this. You know we call Jesus "Emmanuel." That means "God-with-us."
Reader Two	On December 23rd, Ramir's school had a party. Ramir and all the other children were dressed in their best clothes. Everyone brought food to share. There was singing and dancing in the decorated classrooms. When it was time to go home, they all gathered around a wooden box in the hallway. It was filled with straw. A teacher placed a statue of the Infant Jesus in the straw.
Teacher	Let's remember the Child Jesus who came into this world to show God's love for us.
Ramir	(looking at the child) Jesus was born in a barn to a poor family. It was not a perfect world then and it is still not a perfect world. But God is with us and wants us to work together to make a better world.
Reader One	The children sang one more song, then Ramir turned to his schoolmates and exclaimed, "*Maligayang Pasko!* Merry Christmas!"
Everyone	Merry Christmas!

Activities

Our World Booklets

Encourage the children to create booklets on the Philippines.

Discussion Starters

- Talk about what it means to be a "people of God."

- Ask the children if there were times when they felt that God was especially close to them.

- Filipinos celebrate Christmas with great festivity. Discuss what kinds of traditions the children's families celebrate in preparation for Christ's birth.

- In your research on the Philippines, look for a picture of a *parol*. Consider making one in class.

Focusing on Others

A Story from the United States, India, South Korea, the Philippines, Guatemala, and Bolivia

This story, which contrasts the lives of some children from a variety of countries around the world, will help children understand Chapter 2, #30 from *The Church in the Modern World* (paraphrased here):

Change is taking place so very rapidly and in so many areas of our lives that we must be very careful not to become self-centered. We must not base our decisions on what is "good for me," not thinking of how that will affect others. That kind of thinking is called "individualistic morality."

Doing the Groundwork

Before reading this story, bring in books on these countries, start posters for each country, and locate on the map the countries mentioned in this story.

The Story

Choose a narrator, who will read the most lines, and then five more readers.

Narrator	Brian is an eleven-year-old boy who lives in a small city in the United States. Imagine him in gym class at school. Wearing a tee-shirt with the logo of his favorite football team, he bends down to tie his new shoes. The teacher then throws the basketball to him, and the game begins. Later, after a quick hot shower in the locker room, Brian heads to the cafeteria where he buys a soda and gets in line for hot lunch. It is pizza today, and he takes three large pieces. As he gulps down his food, Brian rummages through his backpack to make sure his new calculator is still there.
Reader One	Bhola is an eleven-year-old boy who lives in a village in India. Like Brian, he too is at school. The school building is too small for all the children, so classes are held outside. Bhola sits in the sun with the older students. That way he can be close to the teacher who is writing on the blackboard on the school wall. He feels the sun's intense heat on his head, and also feels the warmth from the other children he sits with, shoulder to shoulder. Gone is the cool feeling he had when he scrubbed down at the well earlier this morning with his brothers.

Bhola's teacher is showing the students math problems. Bhola will have to solve them on his slate later. He wants to make sure he understands how to do them. The school does not have any math or other textbooks.

Narrator   Brian grabs a few of his books, slams his locker shut, and heads out the door with a crowd of students. Inside his bus it is noisy as children shout and tease each other. Brian sighs because the bus is almost full and he will have to share a seat, probably with one of the little kids. He wishes his older sister could have picked him up today. Sometimes she does when she drives the car to her high school. The bus stops at Brian's driveway, and he gets out.

Reader Two   Min-Wha is a twelve-year-old girl who lives in the huge city of Seoul, South Korea. The long school day is over, and she is on her way home to get her violin for her lesson. She gets onto the subway. It is filled with passengers as usual, but everyone has a seat. There is only one seat left. Min-Wha's back-pack is heavy with tonight's homework, so she is glad to sit down. At the next stop, three women get on. Min-Wha immediately stands up and offers her seat to one of the women. Soon the train arrives at Min-Wha's stop. She gets off the subway and walks the remaining streets to her home.

Narrator   Brian unlocks the front door of his house. Everything is quiet. He's hungry, so he puts a bag of popcorn into the microwave. Brian flops down on the family room couch and flips on the television. He watches an old cartoon while he eats the popcorn. Then he goes over to the computer to play a game, taking the television remote control with him so he can flip tv channels. He is engrossed in his game when his mother comes home from work. "I brought some take-out food for dinner," she says. "Your dad is working late, and your sister is at play practice, so they won't be here to eat with us." "My hockey game is at 6:30," Brian reminds her. "I remember," his mom assures him.

Reader Three   Tem-Tem is a ten-year-old boy who lives on one of the many islands that make up the Philippines. He has just walked home from his nearby school, carrying his social studies and math notebooks. School is over for the day. Now it is time to help the family shuck oysters to sell to restaurants. He joins his sister who is already working on the oysters. He hears his mother hum-ming the baby to sleep as a gentle breeze passes through the bamboo house.

Narrator   As Brian and his mother get into their van, his mother yawns. "It's been a long week," she says. Brian looks at her anxiously. "You are staying for the game, aren't you, Mom?" She nods. "Mom, did you remember that tonight we have to turn in our money for the tournament?" "Oh, that's right," she says. "How much?" "Two hundred dollars," Brian answers. His mother's eyebrows go up. She says, "That's a lot of money!" Brian nods and says, "But I really want to play in that tournament! Please, Mom?" "I know," she says, reaching for her purse.

Reader Four   Maria Luisa is a twelve-year-old girl in Guatemala City. Each day she goes with her mother to the city landfill. There they search through rotting food and other garbage, looking for glass, metal, and plastic containers to sell. The money from these recyclables is the only income Maria Luisa's mother has. The hot sun causes the garbage to release poisonous methane gas. "Cover your mouth," her mother says anxiously. But Maria Luisa cannot dig for containers and cover her mouth at the same time. "Watch for broken glass! It's all over. Try not to get cut," her mother cautions. Maria Luisa does the best she can, proud that she can help her mother, but she hates to come to this horrid place. It is difficult to walk, for a person can easily sink into something that has rotted. Maria Luisa pauses to watch a young woman with a baby tied securely on her back. The young mother struggles to pick through the garbage and not lose her balance. "Stay close to me," Maria Luisa's mother says in a low voice. "We will leave soon." Maria Luisa knows that it is reaching the time when the drug addicts and thieves arrive, and her mother is frightened. Maria Luisa moves closer to her, and works on.

Narrator | Home at last after the hockey game, Brian relaxes in the shower. Too tired to even listen to music on his compact disk player, he crawls into bed under the cozy flannel sheet and comforter. He turns out the light next to his bed. The light from his digital clock and the street light near his window give his room a soft glow. Brian stretches himself out in his bed and goes to sleep.

Reader Five | Pedro is a twelve-year-old boy living in the mountains of Bolivia. It is night, and it's very cold. Pedro is tired after a day at the market. Today he went to town with the sacks of potatoes his family raised. After a long, bumpy, and crowded truck ride, he sold all the potatoes at the market. He is glad that his father did not have to go to market and proud that his father is able to depend on him. Shivering now, Pedro crawls into the small bed he shares with his little brother, Pablo. The heavy sheepskin blanket will keep them warm tonight. Still, in his sleep, little Pablo cuddles up to Pedro for more warmth. Outside the cold night is silent. No sounds come from the sheep, cows, or llamas. Everything is quiet inside their adobe home, too, and completely dark. Pedro can still smell the beans and potatoes his mother cooked earlier. Pedro curls himself up under the sheepskin and is soon fast asleep.

Activities

Our World Booklets

There are six countries in this story, including the Philippines, the United States, and Guatemala. Your children may have already made a booklet on the Philippines, and they may make booklets about Guatemala and the United States for upcoming stories. However the other countries—India, South Korea, and Bolivia—will offer plenty of material for booklets for this chapter.

Discussion Starters

For All Ages

- Have youngsters give examples of technology found in this story.

- To better understand the rapid changes in our lives, ask the children to name examples of technology that are part of their childhood but were not part of yours (e.g. personal computers in homes, fax machines, conferencing over the internet, home videos). Name examples of technological advances that were new to their grandparents (e.g. television, frequent air travel, polio vaccine, etc.).

- Discuss the lives of the children in the story. Find the good things and the hardships in each of them.

For Older Children

- Discuss Brian's life. Do the children identify with him, envy him, or think he should change his attitude toward things?

- Define the term "individualistic morality" and use it in your discussions.

- Challenge your youngsters to compare their own lives to the lives of children in the story. In what ways can they focus less on their own wants and more on the needs of others?

- Invite your students to an ongoing challenge: finding examples of "individualistic morality" in the media. They can bring in examples for class discussion.

Hope for Juan

A Story from Guatemala

This story is to help children understand Chapter 2, part 27 of *The Church in the Modern World* (paraphrased here):

The Second Vatican Council stresses a reverence for human life. Each of us must consider all our neighbors—without exception—as another self. We must take into consideration first of all a neighbor's life and what is necessary to live that life with dignity. In this way, we won't be like the rich man who had no concern for the poor man Lazarus.

Doing the Groundwork

Before reading the story, bring in books on Guatemala, start the poster, and locate it on the map.

The Story

In addition to a brief introduction for the teacher to read, you will need two narrators who take turns reading the entire story. The rest of the class joins in on the chorus.

Teacher	In Guatemala, most of the poorest people live in the countryside. However, the majority of the clinics and hospitals are in the cities, so those who live in the country cannot get medical care easily. Also, there is a great shortage of medicines and hospital beds.
Narrator One	High in the mountains of Guatemala, Juan Manuel lay on a small bed in his home, too weak to cry. Mama came in from gathering wild fruits. She came to sit on the dirt floor near him. Looking at him anxiously, she pulled her rosary out of her pocket. "Hail Mary, full of grace, the Lord is with thee..." she prayed quietly.
Narrator Two	When she had finished praying, Mama would put the beans to cook and make the corn tortillas. There would not be enough for everyone to feel full, for this year the crops had been poor. Juan's parents and siblings were all thin now and got sick easily. Juan Manuel, always thin and small, was suffering the most.
Chorus	Mary, mother of us all, please help the children who live and suffer in poverty. Please help the children who live and grow in plenty. Let us see each other as brothers and sisters, and work together so we can all live in peace. Amen.

Narrator One	Someone came to the door. Juan Manuel heard his mother greet Jacinta. She was a catechist who had taught Juan Manuel all about their religion. Soon the friendly, smiling face of Jacinta was looking down at him. "Hola, Juan Manuel! I brought you some juice!" Juan did not answer. He was so sick that nothing mattered anymore.
Narrator Two	The two women began to talk in low voices. "I heard that Juan Manuel was sick, but he is much worse than I expected," Jacinta said gently. "You've done all you can here. Only at a hospital can they help a child this undernourished." Mama began to cry, but said, "Yes, but how can I get him there? My husband left weeks ago to look for work on the plantations on the coast. I can't leave the other children, and soon I can get work picking coffee beans. Maybe then we will have more food." Jacinta said, "He cannot wait that long." Juan Manuel closed his eyes to sleep.
Chorus	Mary, mother of us all, please help the children who live and suffer in poverty. Please help the children who live and grow in plenty. Let us see each other as brothers and sisters, and work together so we all live in peace. Amen.
Narrator One	The next morning, Juan Manuel awoke as his mother wiped his face. Then she began spooning bean broth into his mouth. "You are going to the hospital," she explained. "Jacinta walked all the way over to Tío Tomas' place to ask him to take you. It will take a few hours to get to the hospital. You will stay there until Papa can bring you home, when he is done working at the plantation. Eat a little more now." Juan Manuel swallowed dutifully. He did not want to go, but he had no strength to protest. He looked into his mother's eyes. She was crying but she said, "Remember, I will pray for you each day. We will all be praying for you, and waiting for you to come home. Here comes Tío Tomas now." Juan Manuel's uncle Tomas and cousin Juan Felipe had made a stretcher out of a blanket and two strong, straight tree branches. Mama gently laid Juan Manuel into the stretcher. He was soon on his way down the mountain.
Narrator Two	Tío Tomas talked cheerfully, telling how he and Juan Felipe were going to the coast for work too. They would return with Juan Manuel's father after they had earned some money. "By that time, you will be big and strong and can come home with us," he said. Juan Manuel did not answer. As careful as his uncle and cousin were, he was bounced and bounced in the stretcher until they reached the Red Cross station. There he was placed in a van on the floor, still in the stretcher, for there was no bed in this ambulance. His uncle and cousin jumped in too, Juan Felipe sitting close to his young cousin. The driver was talkative. "You are lucky, my friends," he said. "We were able to get enough gas to get all the way to the hospital."
Chorus	Mary, mother of us all, please help the children who live and suffer in poverty. Please help the children who live and grow in plenty. Let us see each other as brothers and sisters, and work together so we can all live in peace. Amen.

Narrator One	At the hospital, Juan Manuel heard the sound of feet on the cement floor. From his stretcher, he saw white walls. His relatives left, and Juan Manuel was brought to a large room filled with sick children. He was placed into a bed with another child. Someone took his arm, but he was too exhausted to open his eyes. He smelled alcohol, and felt a cool cotton ball washing his arm. Then he felt pain where a needle had entered his arm. "There now, we will get food into you through your veins first. When you're stronger, you will start eating regular food," a voice said. Juan Manuel didn't care. He fell asleep with the needle in his arm.
Narrator Two	The nurse propped Juan Manuel up in bed. She was friendly. "Aren't you looking better! Today we will start giving you soup." Juan Manuel looked around the large room. There were beds everywhere. Smaller children were in white metal cribs, two in each crib. One child was chewing on the rail of a crib. There were flecks of peeling white paint on her lips.
Narrator Two	Juan Manuel smelled medicine and alcohol. Nearby, someone had wet a bed. A baby cried, but no one went to him. The nurses were kind, but much too busy to rock a baby. Some children were staring blankly at the ceiling. One girl with a cast on her leg was silently crying. Flies buzzed around Juan Manuel, and would not leave him alone. The nurses hurried about, changing sheets, feeding children, giving medicine. How he longed to go home! He missed Mama. Did she remember him? He had been gone for so long....
Chorus	Mary, mother of us all, please help the children who live and suffer in poverty. Please help the children who live and grow in plenty. Let us see each other as brothers and sisters, and work together so we all may live in peace. Amen.
Narrator One	A week later, chicken pox spread through the room. All around Juan Manuel, children were dotted with red spots. He heard crying day and night. "Nurse, please come!" a boy called out. Juan Manuel scratched his own pox, turning and tossing with fever. He dreamed of home. When he woke up, he cried.
Narrator Two	Slowly, Juan Manuel's strength returned. Now he wanted to get up, but the nurses could not allow children out of bed. There was no room to play. He looked out the window, wondering where his home was. How long had he been here? Maybe no one would come to get him. Maybe they had forgotten him! Several days later, however, Papa and Tío Tomas arrived. Juan Manuel left the hospital joyfully. Soon he would be home! But he knew he would always remember the lonely, sick children who were still in the hospital.
Chorus	Mary, mother of us all, please help the children who live and suffer in poverty. Please help the children who live and grow in plenty. Let us see each other as brothers and sisters, and work together so we can all live in peace. Amen.

Activities

Our World Booklets

Help children add the Guatemala booklet to their collections.

Discussion Starters

For All Ages

- Have the children imagine what it would be like to be Juan Manuel. Discuss how they might feel, what they might see, etc.

- On the board, have children help you make a list of basic needs (shelter, food, water, medicine, etc.). Then ask if Juan Manuel had these needs met. What changes are needed so that he can get what he needs?

- Also on the board make two categories: NEEDS and WANTS. Discuss the differences. Have children call out items for each list. Which list is longer?

Living with Hunger

A Story from the United States

A story on hunger helps children to understand Chapter 3, #69 of *The Church in the Modern World* (paraphrased here):

All people have the right to a share of earthly goods, enough for themselves and their families. The Church teaches that we are obliged to help the poor because they are our sisters and brothers. We are asked to give more of our possessions than just what is extra.

Doing the Groundwork

Before reading this story, share facts about the United States that your children may not already know. When you make a poster, you may want to add statistics on wealth in this country (found in this story) and after reading the story, add the statistics on hunger and poverty too. Mark the map as usual.

The Story

Before beginning this story, have children look up Matthew 25:35, as they will recite it as the chorus. There are many parts to this story, some being very short. Have Reader One and Reader Two stand on the left side of the room, and the Reporter stand on the right. The other readers for the parts of Teacher, Jessica, Amanda, Father, Mother, Denise, Joan, and Elderly Woman all stand in the center.

Teacher	The United States of America is the wealthiest nation in the world. But as many as fourteen million of its children go to bed hungry at night (one out of five children) because their parents cannot afford to feed their families. Here is a story about hunger in our country.
Reader One	The first class of the day for sixth-grader Denise was math.
Teacher	(handing out math papers) Today's test counts for one third of your grade. You have twenty minutes to complete it.
Reader Two	Denise's stomach rumbled with hunger as she began the first row of math problems. There had been little food at her house last night and this morning. Slowly she did the work, but it was hard to concentrate when she was so hungry.
Reporter	It is harder to recognize who is hungry in the United States than it is in some other countries. Hungry children in our country don't usually die of starvation.

	Instead, they are tired, find it hard to pay attention, and get sick more often than children who have enough food.
Chorus	For I was hungry and you gave me food, I was thirsty and you gave me something to drink. (Matthew 25:35)
Reader One	The lunch room was boisterous with the sounds of children banging trays, dropping silverware, and laughing. Denise sat at a table with some classmates. She was happily eating her free hot lunch. Finally that hollow feeling could go away for a while! Sitting next to Denise was Jessica, a girl who brought cold lunch every day. She looked at Denise's lunch.
Jessica	Those noodles look like worms! And I hate the way that smells. Yuck! I pack my lunch at home because I can't stand the cafeteria food. How can you eat that stuff?
Reader Two	Denise did not have to answer because Amanda spoke up.
Amanda	It all looks good to me. I forgot my lunch money—oh, here comes my dad!
Reader One	Denise watched Amanda's father hurry over to the table.
Father	(handing Amanda a bag from a fast-food restaurant) Here, I figured you'd need something about now!
Amanda	Thanks, Dad! Cheeseburger, fries, and a pie. Great! I'm just starved!
Reader Two	The smell of the french fries wafted over to Denise. She watched Amanda take a bite out of the cheeseburger. Then Denise turned back to the noodle dish on her plate.
Reporter	More that 36 million Americans are poor.
Chorus	I was hungry and you gave me food, I was thirsty and you gave me something to drink.
Reader One	When she reached home after school, Denise let herself in the back door. It was very quiet in the tiny house. Denise wished she had a dog to play with, but Mom said they couldn't afford to feed a dog. Denise also wished the house were nicer, but the landlord wouldn't buy them paint to fix it up. School lunch seemed a long time ago, so Denise went into the kitchen. There was no cereal left in the cupboard, just some graham crackers. The bread bag was empty. There was one egg left, so Denise fried it. Since the bread was gone, she ate graham crackers with it.
Reporter	One in every five children in the United States is poor.
Chorus	I was hungry and you gave me food, I was thirsty and you gave me something to drink.
Reader Two	Denise's mother came home, looking very tired. Still, she was cheerful.
Mother	Hello, my delight! If we hurry, we can catch the five-fifteen bus and get to the food shelf before it closes.
Denise	Oh, Mom, can't we get food like normal people?

Mother	We are normal people, Denise. We are good, hard-working people who can't make enough money to pay for both food and a place to live. What money I have left over after paying rent goes toward the food we can't get at the food shelf. Grab your coat now. I don't want to miss that bus.
Reporter	There are hungry people in all fifty states of the United States.
Chorus	I was hungry and you gave me food, I was thirsty and you gave me something to drink.
Reader One	Everyone was cheerful at the food shelf. A Boy Scout troop had recently held a big food drive and brought in bags and boxes of canned goods. Volunteers were busy sorting them out. Other volunteers were putting cans on shelves. Joan, the food shelf coordinator, called out a greeting.
Joan	Well, here's our friend Denise and her mom! How nice to see you! We've got some good things for you today.
Reader Two	One of the volunteers and Denise's mother began gathering the amount of food they were allowed. Looking around, Denise saw an elderly woman receiving a bag of food. The woman whispered to Joan.
Elderly Woman	Give some of mine to that child over there.
Joan	Thank you, Agnes, you are so generous! But today, we have plenty for both of you!
Reader One	Denise and her mother left. Her mother was carrying a large bag filled with food. Denise was toting a package of oatmeal and a box of dry milk powder. Hurrying down the street, Denise thought about Agnes, who would have gone hungry to help her.
Reporter	At least 2.5 million elderly people experience some hunger each month.
Chorus	I was hungry and you gave me food, I was thirsty and you gave me something to drink.
Reader Two	Back on the bus, Denise's mother closed her eyes while clutching the food bag. Denise looked at her, and then at the other people on the bus. She was so glad to get this food. But her mother worked every day, worked hard to take care of Denise and herself. Why should they have to choose between buying food and paying rent? Why could some kids have pizzas or french fries at school and have nice homes, too? It wasn't fair. Denise propped her chin on the box of powdered milk and stared out the bus window.
Reporter	Of all the wealthy countries in the world, the United States has the highest number of children living in poverty.
Chorus	Dear Jesus, teach us to live in ways that will make it possible for everyone to have the basic needs. Help us to appreciate what we have and show us how to work together so no one goes hungry. Amen.

Activities

Our World Booklets

Help the children make booklets. They can look for similarities and differences between their lives and Denise's.

Discussion Starters

For All Ages

• Following is a list of ten Scripture passages that help us understand what God tells us about food and hunger. Divide the class into ten teams. Each team can look up one of these verses from Scripture, then one child can write it on the board. When all the Scriptures are listed, discuss what each one means. Together write a summary of what the Bible teaches us about attitudes towards food. The Scripture list is:

Genesis 1:29, Leviticus 19:10, Deuteronomy 14:28–29, Proverbs 25:21, Ecclesiastes 8:15, Isaiah 21:14, Luke 3:11, 1 Corinthians 9:4, 1 Timothy 6:8, Hebrews 13:16.

Their Sorrows and Joys Are Ours

A Story from Tanzania, Mexico, Honduras, and Uganda

This story, set in four places in the world, will help children understand a section from Preface #1 of *The Church in the Modern World*, which is:

The joys and hopes, grief and anxieties of the people of our time, especially those who are poor or afflicted, are the joys and hopes, the grief and anxieties of the followers of Christ as well.

Doing the Groundwork

Before reading the story, bring in books on the countries mentioned and start posters. Locate each country on the map. Count up and name all the places you have visited through these stories.

The Story

This story is made up of four segments. Two are based on true stories. The information for the story of Lupita is from the April 2000 issue of *Maryknoll* magazine, pages 32-36. The information for Pepe's story is from the June 2000 issue, pages 20-21. The other two stories have fictional characters, but are based on real circumstances.

Before reading the story, ask the children to silently remember times in their lives when they felt joy, grief, anxiety, and hope. For this story, you will need seven readers and a prayer leader.

Reader One   Esta was twenty-eight years old and the mother of three children. Growing up in her Tanzanian village, she had never learned to read and write. Now her children were beginning to learn these skills, and she was determined not to be left behind. Once a week, Esta walked three miles in the afternoon heat to attend a class taught by a missioner. There she worked hard and asked many questions.

Reader Two   One day, Esta came home to their hut made of wooden poles covered with dried cow dung, and a grass roof. Instead of starting to make the *engurma*, the thick maize porridge they would have for the next meal, she called her children to her. She was smiling, and her eyes were bright. "Watch!" she said, opening a notebook. She began to write. The children stood near, not making a sound. When Esta finished, she began to read what she had written, "Salome, Daniel, and Tumaini, Esta's children." Then she looked up into the shining faces of her children. "Mama, Mama, you can read!" Daniel exclaimed, clapping his hands. "Mama can write, too!" Salome shouted. Tumaini, too young to understand, jumped up and down with joy, too. Esta put her arms out and all three children tumbled into them.

Teacher: Invite two or three children to tell their own stories of joyful moments.

Prayer Leader and Chorus	Holy Spirit, help us share the joys, griefs, worries, and hopes of others. And give us the wisdom to know when to help them. Amen.
Reader Three	Lupita is thirteen years old. She lives in a small village in Mexico with her aunt and two sisters. If you were to visit her, she would show you pictures of her family. And she would share her sadness. In 1997, there was a war between the army and some rebels. One day the villagers were in their chapel, praying for peace. Suddenly, soldiers burst in and began shooting! Lupita's mother and father were both killed. So were her sisters Rosa, Veronica, Antonia, Micaela, and Juana. Two other sisters, Lucia and Ernestina, were badly wounded. In all, forty-five people were killed that day. Fifty-four other village children were orphaned, and many were injured.
Reader Four	After Lupita has shown you the pictures of her family, she would show you a statue of the Virgin Mary. It too was hit by a bullet that day. The surviving villagers lovingly bandaged the statue which still stands in the chapel. "She is one of us," Lupita says, gently touching the statue.

Teacher: Perhaps you will need a moment of silence at this point. Make a judgment whether it is appropriate to ask a child to share a story of grief, or to go on to the prayer.

Prayer Leader and Chorus	Holy Spirit, help us share the joys, griefs, worries, and hopes of others. And give us the wisdom to know when to help them. Amen.
Reader Five	All his life, all two years of it, Pepe has lived with the destruction that Hurricane Mitch left behind. This terrible storm hit Guatemala, Honduras, El Salvador, and Nicaragua in 1998, leaving thousands of families without homes, food, or work. Now little Pepe's mother has a job in a factory, helping rebuild her family's life while rebuilding their country of Honduras.
Reader Six	Little Pepe does not know anything but this poverty. But when his mother leaves for work, Pepe knows he is left behind all by himself. He sits down by a tree, and begins to cry and wail. Later, he will wander the streets. The neighbors will look after him, giving him scraps of food. When Pepe's mother is done working, she will come and find him. But right now, Pepe is scared and alone. All he wants is his mother's arms around him.

Teacher: Invite one or more students to share stories of times when they were worried or frightened.

Prayer Leader and Chorus	Holy Spirit, help us share the joys, griefs, worries, and hopes of others. And give us the wisdom to know when to help them. Amen.

Reader Seven	It was crowded and noisy in the clinic in northern Uganda. Among the local mothers and children were doctors and nurses from many parts of the world. They had come to Uganda as part of a program called Doctors Without Borders. A seven-year-old boy sat nervously on an examining table. Nearly blind, he didn't see a young French doctor approaching him. "Hello," she greeted him softly. "I am going to examine your eyes now." The boy's mother stood nearby, watching tensely. When the exam was over, the doctor patted the child's shoulder and said, "His blindness has not gone too far. I am almost certain we can restore his sight!" The doctor smiled as the hopeful mother and son hugged each other.
Prayer Leader and Chorus	Holy Spirit, help us share the joys, griefs, worries, and hopes of others. And give us the wisdom to know when to help them. Amen.

Teacher: Invite two students to share their stories of hope.

Activities

Our World Booklets

With this story, students can focus on one topic for each country, comparing their lives with those in the story within that topic. Suggested topics are education and types of schools for Esta's story, personal loss for Lupita's story, recovery after a natural disaster for Pepe's story, and medical care for children for the Ugandan child's story.

Discussion Starters

- To live justly, we must have empathy for others. Help the children define empathy.

- Discuss times when someone empathized with them. Talk about what would have happened if that person had not shown empathy.

- Name different jobs where empathy is essential (a few examples: medical workers, teachers, parents, those in religious life, those who work with the elderly or handicapped, firefighters). Discuss what might happen if those people did not have empathy.

- Remind children that as Christians, they are called to empathize with others. Have a follow-up discussion a week later about children's recent experiences of showing empathy.

PART THREE

Exploring the Principles of Catholic Social Teaching

Stories of People Who Act Justly

Introduction

Catholic social teachings are essential elements of our faith. Rooted deep in the history of Christianity, from the Hebrew prophets to Jesus himself, these teachings are based on the Scriptures, which proclaim a strong commitment to those who are poor. This commitment is linked to our understanding of human life and human dignity. We encounter these social teachings when we worship, in the homily and the reading of the Scriptures.

What can these teachings accomplish?

- They can inspire us to consider the principles of justice and to develop an awareness of situations of injustice.

- They can strengthen us to take a stand for justice in our families, local communities, and in the greater society.

- They can teach us how to bring about changes that affirm the sacredness and dignity of human persons.

Since the publication of Pope Leo XIII's social encyclical, *On the Condition of Workers* in 1891, many papal letters, council and synod documents, and statements by the U.S. Catholic bishops have furthered social justice by stating Church teachings concisely and encouraging us to incorporate them into our lives. As teachers and parents we need to present them to our children, so that these teachings influence their life choices.

This section describes the principles as they are often presented, and offers stories of people who exemplify them.

Using Part Three

An explanation of one principle will precede each story. The stories themselves will introduce children to real people who are role models because they strive to live justly. Most of the stories are contemporary. Suggestions for discussion follow.

As these themes are often found in children's literature, suggestions of picture and chapter books that reflect these principles are also listed.

Ongoing Project

Begin compiling a book on people working for social justice. The following stories will help you get started, but the project can go on indefinitely. Collect newspaper, magazine, and internet articles about people working for justice, as well as stories about projects and movements for justice. Place the articles and photos in a scrap book. You may want to identify each of them with principles of social teaching and label them on the pages. The idea is to compile a collection that will inspire children to become involved and to better understand the issues. In addition to people mentioned in these stories, suggest that children look for information on Pope John Paul II, Kofi Annan, Mother Teresa, Jimmy Carter, Oscar Romero, Martin Luther King, Mahatma Gandhi, Ruby Bridges, Nelson Mandela, Dorothy Day, and Fred Rogers. Bring in mission magazines. Search newspapers for recent events. Look locally, in your community, school, or parish for examples. Refer to the organizations in Part Four for types of justice work. Convey the idea to children that they can continually find examples of people who act justly.

Operation: New Homes for Orphans

A Story of the Holt Family

The Principle

The human person is central in Catholic social teaching. Each person has a dignity that comes from God, a dignity rooted in the fact that each of us is made in God's image. Humans are the best reflection of God's presence among us. Each person, no matter who they are and what they accomplish, has infinite worth. People are more important than things.

The Story

The following story tells of an extraordinary family whose strong belief in the sacredness of the human person led them to undertake a project that would ultimately affect thousands of people. This information is taken from *The Seed from the East* by Mrs. Harry Holt, as told to David Wisner (1956, 1986). You will need an adult narrator and two readers. You could display the chorus words on the blackboard so everyone can easily join in.

Narrator	In the 1950s, there was a war in the country of Korea that left many children orphaned. They suffered greatly, especially the children who had had an American father and a Korean mother. This is the story of one family in Oregon who heard about their pain. They believed that each person is precious, and found a way to help that would eventually affect thousands of people.
Reader One	In Korea, more than forty-five years ago, rubble from large buildings filled the streets because of a war. Houses were burned down. People had no choice but to drink bad water, which made them sick. Children got whooping cough and other illnesses, but little medicine was available. Everyone was hungry. Families had been separated during the war, and many people had died.
	One day, a soldier driving a jeep saw movement by a garbage heap. He looked again. Could it possibly be a baby? He stopped the jeep and ran to the garbage. The place smelled bad but the soldier heard a weak cry so he kept looking. Yes, there was a baby! She was so thin her arms were like sticks, and she was dirty and cold. He wrapped his jacket around her. Could this little one survive even a few hours? The soldier doubted it, but still he must try and help her.
Chorus	Jesus, please help us see the holiness in each person.

Reader Two	At about the same time in Oregon, in a beautiful valley, a farm spread across many acres. Here the Holt family lived—Harry and Bertha and their six children, Stewart, Wanda, Molly, Barbara, Suzanne, and Linda. They raised cows, sheep, and horses, and planted wheat and other crops. A big dog named Jumbo romped on the lawn in front of the large house. The younger children went to school and took piano lessons, and they all worked hard on the farm. They always prayed together at each meal.
Chorus	Jesus, please help us see the holiness in each person.
Reader One	Many orphanages in Korea were good, but others had very few supplies. Often babies were fed only rice water. Many children like the one the soldier had found were brought in, so the supplies had be to stretched even further. Missionaries from the United States sent home pictures and movies about the Korean orphans, hoping for help from Americans.
Chorus	Jesus, please help us see the holiness in each person.
Reader Two	Suzanne Holt came home from school one day in the autumn and told her mother, "A man will be in town tomorrow to show a movie about orphaned Korean children." The family watched the movie and vowed to help in some way. "Each little one is so precious, each one is a gift! We must do something!" said Bertha. The family agreed. After much prayer, Bertha and Harry decided they would adopt eight children! No one had ever brought children from Korea to the United States to be adopted. Harry would go to Korea to find the children himself.
Chorus	Jesus, please help us see the holiness in each person.
Reader One	In Korea, Harry saw many children who needed food, medicine, and love. He prayed, asking God to guide him. One by one, he found children he felt God wanted him to adopt. He named them Joe, Betty, Mary, Nathaniel, Paul, Christine, Helen, and Bob. They lived together in a little room. Harry fed them, changed diapers, sang songs, and gave them medicine. As he did so, he prayed that he could find a way to help all the others he could not adopt.
Chorus	Jesus, please help us see the holiness in each person.
Reader Two	In Oregon, Bertha and the older children fed the cows, harvested the wheat, and picked the apples. And, they made piles of tiny dresses, pajamas, shirts, pants, and bibs for all the little ones they were waiting for. Every day they prayed for their new brothers and sisters, calling them each by name.
Chorus	Jesus, please help us see the holiness in each person.
Reader Two	People in Oregon learned that Harry Holt was in Korea trying to adopt children. They called Bertha, asking if Harry could bring other children to join their families. Bertha was delighted. Perhaps this was the answer to Harry's prayer! But she also knew Harry was having a hard time getting passports for the eight children. How could they help others if they could not even get the first eight home? Bertha soon found a way. She wrote to her representatives in

	Congress. She asked that the United States government pass a special law saying Harry could bring the children to Oregon and adopt them.
Chorus	Jesus, please help us see the holiness in each person.
Reader One	After several long months and much work by people on both sides of the world, the law was passed. Harry was coming home with his eight new children! And he was bringing four more children for other families who wanted to adopt orphans, too. It was a busy plane trip with that many babies, bottles, and diapers! Other people helped him, and they too came to love these little children.
Chorus	Jesus, please help us see the holiness in each person.
Reader Two	The Holts' big house now sheltered sixteen people. High chairs and cribs filled the rooms, and eight tiny pairs of cowboy boots were lined up before bedtime. Guests arrived, wanting to meet the babies. Television, newspaper, and radio people came to take pictures and ask questions. Letters poured in and the phone rang all day. People who wanted to adopt children asked for help. Harry was glad to be home. He kept praying for all the children still in hospitals and orphanages in Korea.
Chorus	Jesus, please help us see the holiness in each person.
Narrator	In the following years, the Holts set up an adoption agency that worked in Korea and from their Oregon home. They built an orphanage in Korea so thousands of orphaned children could become part of families in other countries. Although there had already been international adoptions after World War II, the Holts were the first to work with Korea. They began a major movement with many agencies and thousands of children. Today, the orphanage the Holts built has become a huge place. It serves children in many ways, including children who are mentally and physically challenged. Because of Harry and Bertha's vision of international adoption, now orphaned children from all over the world find families and homes. They are helped by people who honor the sacred dignity of each and every child.

Discussion Starters

After explaining the principle, use these questions to help children develop a broader vision of what it means

- Why are people more important than things?

- In addition to material things, what other things might mistakenly be considered more important than people? Winning? Money? Accomplishments?

- What groups do you participate in? How do these groups show respect for each person?

- Watch/listen to commercials on television, on the radio, and in the print media for advertising that respects/violates this principle.

- Do our celebrations of Christmas and birthdays reflect a belief in the sacredness of the person?

- What does this principle of respect for the sacredness and dignity of each person teach us about abortion? Euthanasia? Capital punishment?

Suggestions for Finding this Theme in Children's Literature

Picture Books

Hope by Isabell Monk

Amazing Grace by Mary Hoffman

Mrs. Katz and Tush by Patricia Polacco

A Baker's Portrait by Michelle Edwards

People by Peter Spier

Horton Hears a Who by Dr. Seuss

Early Chapter Books

Sadako and the 1000 Paper Cranes by Eleanor Coerr

Hundred Dresses by Eleanor Estes

Chapter Books

The Education of Little Tree by Forrest Carter

If It Hadn't Been for Yoon Jun by Marie G. Lee

Sojourner Truth, Ain't I a Woman? Patricia and Frederick McKissack

A Truly Royal Family

A Story of Margaret and Malcolm of Scotland

The Principle

We are social beings. While some of us are more inclined towards socializing than others, we all have a natural affinity for relationships. It is through other people, through our experiences in a community, that we first come to know ourselves and to understand our dignity and our rights. The foremost community, the basic cell of society, is the family. It is also within the family that we learn and first act on our values. The family, then, is capable of making major contributions to issues of social justice.

From the family, we move out to the broader community. Family members have the right and responsibility to contribute to communities in society. Government and other institutions that guide political and economic life are instruments to protect the rights of and promote the well-being of individuals and families. If basic human needs are not met by the greater society and its institutions, Catholics are called into action, to work through government to meet these needs.

In summary, we are a community people in both the personal and public aspects of our lives. Like Sarah and Abraham before us, we are called to be a people of God. We must live fully and nurture our family life, and act publicly to ensure the healthy life of everyone in community.

The Story

Long before the term Catholic social teaching was in use, a family in the eleventh century was living out the call to family and community. This was no ordinary family. The father was King Malcolm of Scotland. His wife, the queen, became known as Saint Margaret, patron of Scotland. One of their daughters became a beloved queen of England. Three of their sons became kings of Scotland, one of whom was revered as a saint. Their greatness lies not in their royal status, however, but in their actions. You will need five readers for this story.

Reader One   Princess Matilda entered her mother's room quietly. She saw that Queen Margaret was praying, so she waited. In her mother's hands was a jeweled prayer book. Matilda knew that her father, King Malcolm, had had those jewels put on the prayer book because he loved her mother so much. That had been before Matilda was born, before her father learned about the Christian faith.

With Margaret's help, Malcolm had become a prayerful man and a wonderful king. Working together, they had churches built for their country of Scotland. They brought in teachers and artists, and held important religious meetings. The king often asked for the queen's advice when he made decisions. The princess also knew that her parents prayed together each day. They went to Mass frequently and also prayed with Matilda, her sister, and six brothers.

The princess smiled as she thought of her fierce-looking but gentle father, of her tender and strong mother, and all those brothers and her sister. Now the queen closed her prayer book and smiled at Matilda. "Yes, dear?" she asked.

Reader Two   Matilda said, "Our tutor says to tell you that we are finished with our work, Mama." The queen had brought in excellent teachers from England for her children, but she herself taught them religion classes. Queen Margaret carefully placed the jeweled prayer book on a special shelf. "Then I will come. I just finished praying for your brother David. I pray for each of you every day. Matilda, I think it is time you started going with me on my outside work. Tomorrow you can come. Dress warmly!"

Reader Three   Some hours later, Princess Matilda went down the cold castle hallway to the dining room. It was a large room, built for royal banquets. Matilda knew it was most often used by people who were not royal. Every night of Advent and Lent, her parents welcomed the hungry of their kingdom into the castle. The princess watched from the doorway. Tables were filled with at least two hundred people in ragged clothing. She looked down the aisles. There was her mother with a large kettle in her arms. She was going down one row, ladling soup and talking in her gracious way. In another aisle, the king was doing the same. There was a big smile on his face as he talked with his subjects. Matilda watched all this, knowing her mother had also prepared food for orphaned children that day.

Reader Four   The next morning, the children's nurse was pulling layer after layer of clothing over Princess Matilda's head. Matilda began squirming. "You must dress warmly!" the nurse insisted. "The queen said so and anyone with any brains listens to the queen. What a wise woman! What a blessed child you are to have such parents! Now off you go, to learn your mother's work!"

Reader Five   The wind was biting cold but Matilda enjoyed feeling royal. She was riding her pony next to her mother's horse. Two strong knights rode with them. Her mother spoke quietly to her as they went along. "At the next house, a new baby has been born, and the older children are sick. We will leave some warm clothing and medicine." From place to place they went, helping and praying with the poor families. Her mother was always a teacher even as she was the Queen. On the way home, Matilda felt the cold seeping into her cloak as she sat upon the pony. Their group met a woman, poorly dressed for the cold. She was shivering as she trudged along. "Stop," the queen said. "I want to give her my cloak." Princess Matilda watched her mother take off her woolen cloak and offer it to the woman. Then they rode on. Matilda turned a moment to watch the woman walking swiftly now, bundled up in the warm cloak. The princess vowed that if she ever became a queen, she would try to be as good to her children and her people as Queen Margaret.

Discussion Starters

After explaining the principle, use these questions to help children develop a broad vision of what it means:

- How do babies learn to trust?

- What do family members do each day to help each other?

- What have you learned in your family about how to treat others?

- How do families reach out to those outside of their group?

- Discuss different types of families, emphasizing that there are many ways people can make a family (e.g., grandparents, single parent families, adoptive families).

- How does our government help and protect families?

- Discuss a variety of ways people help, such as music teachers, coaches, firefighters, librarians, doctors and nurses, social workers, food shelf organizers.

Suggesting for Finding this Theme in Children's Literature

Picture Books

Dogger by Shirley Hughes

Baseball Saved Us by Ken Mochizuki

Thunder Cake by Patricia Polacco

Miss Rumphius by Barbara Cooney

The Doorbell Rang by Pat Hutchins

Chapter Books

All-of-a-Kind Family series by Sydney Taylor

Because of Winn-Dixie by Kate De Camillo

Anne of Green Gables by L.M. Montgomery

Maniac Magee by Jerry Spinelli

Little House Series by Laura Ingalls Wilder

An Artist With a Mission

A Story of Kathe Schmidt Kollwitz

The Principle

The dignity of human persons stems from our relationship with God. This dignity comes with rights and responsibilities. We each are entitled to the things that make life truly human: shelter, work, education, clothing, food, health care, freedom of conscience, religious liberty, the right to raise a family, to immigrate, to be free of unfair discrimination, and to have sufficient goods for family and self. These things are essential for human beings if we are to realize our dignity.

With rights come responsibilities. Because we are social beings, to live means to be united with others. So, we are responsible to see that the rights of others are observed. We are responsible for our families, for our immediate community, and for the larger society. We each must work for the common good. In the Old Testament, the Jews were instructed to imitate the loving justice God had shown them. Jesus' ministry followed this tradition. He began by fulfilling Isaiah's prophecy (Isaiah 61:1–2): "The Spirit of the Lord is upon me, because he has anointed me to proclaim release to the captives and recovery of sight to the blind, to let the oppressed go free" (Luke 4:18).

The balance of rights and responsibilities is crucial. Without rights, the person is sacrificed to those with greater power. Without responsibilities, our rights lead to selfish practices.

The Story

Kathe Schmidt Kollwitz (1867-1945) was one of the greatest artists of the twentieth century. She held strong beliefs about the rights of humans, ideals she developed as a child. She used her artistic talents and vision to call attention and compassion to those whose rights had been taken from them, fulfilling the responsibility she felt toward the downtrodden. If possible, show children examples of her art, choosing what you feel is appropriate. Children can draw scenes from her life as depicted in the following story, which could be shown as the story is read. You will need six readers.

Reader One   The little girl, Kathe, sat by her father, listening as he read poems about poor people he saw every day. Though these people worked hard, they never had enough food, or warm places to live, he said. Their children were hungry and cold, too, and many could not go to school. As Kathe listened, she imagined men pulling their plows themselves for they had no horses. She pictured mothers holding sick children, helpless for they had no medicine. She imagined the anger on the faces of these suffering people. Then her grandfather began speaking and her mother and brother joined in. Kathe listened to them speak about their concern for others who did not have what her family had. Sometimes she realized they were talking about things she had read about already.

Reader Two   Kathe's parents took great pride in their children. One of their hopes was that the children would understand the injustices of the world and take part in political activities. Kathe and her little sister often walked down by the docks of their city to watch the workers there. Kathe remembered all the discussions and poems she had heard. Watching those who had so little touched her heart.

Reader Three   Kathe's parents also wanted their children to develop their talents. It was clear from early on that one of Kathe's greatest gifts was art. Her parents made certain she got the best art training a woman could have at the time. She developed an extraordinary talent for drawing. She also made sculptures and lithographs. Her art showed others how strongly she felt about those who had less and those who were treated unfairly.

Reader Four   When Kathe was older, she married a man named Karl Kollwitz. Karl was a doctor who took care of the very people Kathe cared about. In their home in Berlin, Germany, they had a doctor's office for Karl and a studio for Kathe. Through Karl's work, Kathe came to know the people she drew. When Kathe and Karl had children, Kathe began to understand better how hard the poor mothers worked to protect their children. Often the mothers themselves lacked safety and shelter.

Kathe drew and sculpted. Through her art she depicted the problems of those who did not have work, who were sick, who were hungry, who were unfairly imprisoned. Her paintings and sculptures were powerful. Many people loved her work, even though it made them sad. Her pictures made them think about the rights and responsibilities they had.

Reader Five   Then, a terrible war started which we call World War I. Kathe's son, Peter, told her he wanted to join the army. Kathe agreed, but soon regretted it because not long after, young Peter was killed. Kathe mourned for years. Sometimes she could not work. Other times, she made forceful sculptures and prints of mothers loving their children. Years after Peter's death, she sculpted a war memorial of parents grieving for their sons lost in war. She and her husband were the models for the statues she sculpted. Through that memorial, she wanted to show that the young soldiers who died were denied their most important right: to live out their lifetimes.

Reader Six   When Kathe was more than seventy years old, another terrible war began. The Nazis were in power in Kathe's town of Berlin. They controlled everything, including what art could be shown. They decided Kathe's work could not be seen. Karl died, and their grandson, also named Peter, was killed in this war. For the last years of her life, Kathe lived quietly. Even though her art was not displayed, she kept drawing. Kathe believed that each person must take responsibility for others. "The culture of a whole nation can...be built upon nothing else," she said. Kathe died just before World War II ended. Her sculptures and drawings go on speaking for her, calling for justice for every person.

Discussion Starters

These concepts present a challenge to teachers and parents because they oppose much of present-day culture, where individual pleasures and possessions are portrayed so alluringly in the media. After explaining the principle, start a discussion by making a list of rights and responsibilities for all the children to see. Use the following questions:

- Are you and most of the people you know able to exercise these rights?

- Choose one of the rights listed. Discuss how your life would be different if that right was taken from you.

- Research the lifestyle of different peoples around the world (mission magazines will be helpful here). Do these people enjoy the rights mentioned? If not, what are the consequences?

- Name some examples of well-known people, organizations and churches, and governments who work to make sure that people's rights are protected.

Suggestions for Finding this Theme in Children's Literature

Picture Books

Thank-you, Mr. Falker by Patricia Polacco
The Butterfly by Patricia Polacco
Young Martin's Promise by Walter Dean Myers
Jamaica's Find by Juanita Havill

Older Picture Book

Pink and Say by Patricia Polacco

Chapter Books

Charlotte's Web by E.B. White
One-Eyed Cat by Paula Fox
Behind the Bedroom Wall by Laura Williams
Who Comes with Cannons? by Patricia Beatty
Good Night, Mr. Tom by Michelle Magorian
Shades of Gray by Carolyn Reeder

Children Freeing Children

A Story of Craig Kielburger

The Principle

Our Catholic tradition calls upon us to give preferential treatment to those who are poor and vulnerable. Long ago, our Jewish ancestors were instructed not to harvest their crops completely, but to leave the gleanings for the widowed, the orphaned, and the stranger (Leviticus 19:9–10, Deuteronomy 24:19–22). They were to remember that they had been slaves once, and were led out of slavery by God's love. They were to treat others with the same generosity God had shown them. Jesus also made this very clear in Matthew 25. He said that God will judge us based on our response to human need. He instructed, "For I was hungry and you gave me food, I was thirsty and you gave me something to drink."

Our response to those in need must go beyond acts of mercy to acts of justice. Our faith insists that the poor are owed a share of our wealth. It is not simply an act of generosity but a requirement of the gospel. This is echoed in the Catechism of the Catholic Church: "Those who are oppressed by poverty are the object of a preferential love on the part of the church" (*Catechism #2448*).

The Story

The following story tells of one child's efforts to assist poor and exploited children, who are among the most vulnerable of people. It can be read by one narrator or by seven readers. You might want to have the children draw pictures for each of the scenes described, then make booklets or a mural out of them.

Narrator   This is a story of a journey. It is about a seven-week trip a Canadian boy made to South Asia. But a journey is more than a trip. He began his journey as a secure, happy child. He came to learn about children his own age whose lives were extremely difficult. Eventually he started working for children's rights.

People often take pictures when they travel. As we listen to this story, let's imagine what the pictures of this boy might be like.

First Picture   Imagine a breakfast table in a house in Toronto, Canada. It was April 1995, a sunny Wednesday. Twelve-year-old Craig Kielburger reached for the newspaper. He liked to read the comics every day. This morning, however, he saw a story on the front page that changed his life forever. Craig read about a boy in Pakistan who had been forced to work in a carpet factory. The boy was chained to a loom where he tied thousands of tiny knots to form carpets. He was forced to work twelve hours a day, six days a week, for three cents a day. After six years, the boy escaped and began telling news reporters about this child slavery. When the boy died a few years later, many people suspected that he was killed by the factory owners. These owners did not want the world to know they were using children for forced labor.

Craig was horrified. He had never heard of anything like this before. Now he was determined to learn everything he could. Craig had difficulty concentrating at school that day. After school he headed to the library to gather information on child labor.

Second Picture

Picture Craig that evening, poring over articles he had found at the library. He learned that in some countries, children younger than he were forced to work in underground mines, in fireworks factories, or as servants for rich people. Sometimes, like the boy in the newspaper, they had to work in carpet factories. These children rarely attended school, and were underpaid and underfed. Much of the work was unhealthy or dangerous. Craig was furious with the world for letting children suffer so much! Was there anything he could do? He began to plan.

Third Picture

Now picture Craig setting up an office in his house. He called human rights organizations to receive information. Then he told his friends everything he learned. Soon they formed an organization of children against child labor. They called it Free the Children. Members spoke in schools about child labor. They spoke with government officials, asking them to provide more education and protection for children. More and more children joined Free the Children. Many more speeches were made. Thousands of letters were written.

Fourth Picture

Imagine a picture of Craig standing at his fax machine. A report comes in about an explosion in a fireworks factory in Rhotak, India. Twelve workers, all children, were killed. Dozens more were injured. Craig immediately sent copies of this report to the mayor of Toronto, asking if Free the Children could speak to the city council. The council agreed never to allow fireworks made by children into Toronto. Craig understood now that he and his friends could accomplish a lot, but they needed to learn more. He must travel to the places where child labor is most common: Bangladesh, Thailand, India, Nepal, and Pakistan. His parents agreed to the trip after UNICEF found places for him to stay. Craig found a trustworthy guide who would be with him for the entire trip.

Fifth Picture

Picture Craig as he arrived in South Asia. He saw much beauty and happiness. But he also saw poor children working as porters at train stations, loading cargo onto ships, mending fishnets, and cleaning fish. There were children selling fruit or flowers or bagging candy. Craig was angered to see children breaking bricks and using dangerous machinery. Craig was particularly bothered when he saw a girl sorting through used medical syringes. These needles were covered with hazardous germs. He saw children working in a fireworks factory. Some of them were scarred from explosions.

Sixth Picture	Craig met Mother Teresa, who encouraged his work. He also met with the Prime Minister of Canada who was also traveling in South Asia. When it was time to go home, Craig was sad to leave. He wondered what he should do next. His friend and guide, Alam, told him that everything has a solution. "You must live your own life to reflect that solution," he said.

Craig met with adults who were trying to help these children. When they were able to rescue several boys from slavery in a carpet factory, Craig helped them return home. He watched the parents weep as they embraced their sons. They had feared they would never see their children again.

Sixth Picture	Craig met Mother Teresa, who encouraged his work. He also met with the Prime Minister of Canada who was also traveling in South Asia. When it was time to go home, Craig was sad to leave. He wondered what he should do next. His friend and guide, Alam, told him that everything has a solution. "You must live your own life to reflect that solution," he said.
Seventh Picture	Picture Craig today, still working to bring an end to the problem of child labor. He said, "As citizens of the world, we are all responsible for one another." Picture Free the Children growing into an organization of children in many countries. Picture children being freed to go to school and to live with their families. And picture yourself becoming involved in helping other children who are still not free.

For more information on Free the Children, see Part Four.

Discussion Starters

- Start a discussion by having children list people they think are the most needy and powerless in their community, in this country, in the world.

- Have the children research and report on examples in history when the poor and vulnerable have been helped or ignored. Stories of saints such as John Bosco and Frances of Rome will be helpful for this project.

- Ask youngsters if they believe that they can bring about changes to help the persons who are most needy and powerless. Brainstorm some possible ways.

Suggestions for Finding this Theme in Children's Literature

Picture Books

The Quiltmaker's Gift by Jeff Brumbeau and Gail de Marcken
How Many Days to America? by Eve Bunting
Fly Away Home by Eve Bunting

Early Chapter Books

Meet Addy, An American Girl by Connie Porter
Changes for Samantha, An American Girl by Valerie Tripp

Chapter Books

The Great Gilly Hopkins by Katherine Paterson
The Girl-Son by Anne E. Neuberger
So Far from Home, The Diary of Mary Driscoll, an Irish Mill Girl by Barry Denenberg (Dear America Series)
I Thought My Soul Would Rise and Fly, The Diary of Patsy, a Freed Girl by Joyce Hansen (Dear America Series)

Cesar's Strike for Justice

A Story of Cesar Chavez

The Principle

Work is often seen simply as a way to make a living. While this is essential, work is more than that. It is an expression of our dignity, and it is our way of participating in God's creative action. Catholic social teaching views work in this positive light. It also claims that people have a right to decent and productive work. Workers have a right to fair wages and to private property. The Catholic Church supports workers in choosing to form or join unions or worker associations that contribute to their dignity and rights. The economy exists to serve people, not the other way around.

The Story

One man who spent his life fighting for the dignity and fair treatment of workers was Cesar Chavez. Before reading this story, briefly explain to children who migrant workers are and what their work is. Also, explain the use of picket signs during a strike. Have four children make four picket signs with the phrases noted below. As you narrate the story, pause at each of these phrases. Have one child hold up the picket sign while another child reads the information. You will need four children to hold the signs and four to read.

Narrator | Ten-year-old Cesar Chavez was used to work. On his family farm in Arizona, he pulled weeds and carried water to nourish melons, peppers, corn, and beans. It was a hard but good life, for the family loved and took care of each other. Now, however, the farm had been sold. Like many people who lived during the Depression of the 1930s, the Chavez family was unable to pay their taxes. The parents and their six children moved to California. They began looking for work on the large fruit and vegetable farms there. They hoped the children would not have to work, but would be able to go to school. Cesar hoped to buy a pair of shoes. When they arrived at one farm, they found shacks made of sheet metal. Cesar looked at his mother. Was this where they were going to live?

First Picket Sign | Better Living Conditions for Farm Workers

Some farms had housing for the farm workers: one-room shacks made out of sheet metal. These shacks were like ovens in the summer heat. There were no windows to let out heat or let in light. There was no running water or indoor toilets. Blankets had to be spread on the floor for there were no beds. Other farms did not even have this kind of "housing." Whole families slept in tents or cars. Often they went hungry. Their work produced food for others, but the workers made so little money they did not have enough to eat. Because the families had to move from job to job, the children often could not go to school.

Narrator | Cesar and his family began their lives as farm workers. All day long, the sun blazed as they stooped over, weeding or harvesting food. At night they slept on the floor of the hot shack. Often they were hungry, always they were tired. They moved from place to place, looking for work all over California. One winter they had no work, so they lived under a bridge. With all the moving around, Cesar attended three dozen schools by eighth grade.

He would never go beyond that grade, for Cesar's father was hurt in a car accident. Cesar began working full-time in the fields to take his place. He worked in the vineyards, tending grapes. His back ached, insects swarmed over him, and the sun beat down. Miserable as he was, Cesar thought about all the families he had met who were as poor as he was. He thought about the times he was mistreated because he was Mexican-American. He remembered his mother's gentle advice never to be violent. He knew generations of his family had always helped other people. Cesar longed to do something that would change things for the better.

Second Picket Sign | Better Working Conditions for the Farm Workers

Workers planted, weeded, and harvested foods like lettuce, grapes, strawberries, and peas. To do this they had to work many hours in the hot sun without any rest time. The only drinking water provided by the growers was miles away from the fields. Workers were only allowed to use short-handled hoes. That meant they had to bend over to work all day long. This caused back pain and injuries.

Narrator | In the following years, Cesar worked to help Spanish-speaking people to learn English and to register to vote. He knew they would have more influence then. He tried, but failed, to get the farm owners to treat farm workers better. Many people respected this soft-spoken, gentle, religious man. Soon, they would see his great courage and inner strength.

Third Picket Sign | Farm Workers Are Being Cheated

The farm workers were often paid according to the amount of food they had picked. The baskets they filled were weighed to figure their wages. However, often those doing the weighing wrote down the numbers incorrectly. This way they cheated the workers out of some of the money they had worked so hard to earn. Also, to find work, farm workers had to talk with a labor contractor instead of with the farm owners. Often the labor contractor paid the farm workers only enough money to buy food. They promised to pay them the rest of the money when the job was finished. However, when the job was done, the labor contractor could not be found. The farm worker family was then

	cheated out of wages for days of work. They would go hungry.
Narrator	With the help of a man named Fred Ross, Cesar learned to organize workers so they could help each other and demand fair treatment. He was an excellent leader and many workers joined. They called themselves the National Farm Workers Association. They decided to strike—to refuse to work until they got what they needed. The strike was against grape growers, who were very powerful. It lasted five years! Cesar gave speeches, encouraged others, and made plans the whole time. Sometimes they marched through cities, carrying picket signs. Their feet were raw from the long walks. Sometimes they prayed near fields of grapes, holding banners with pictures of Our Lady of Guadalupe. Cesar fasted for many days to gain attention for their cause. Sometimes strikers were hurt by angry people, but they followed Cesar's example of not fighting back. People who were not farm workers began joining the strikers. The numbers grew. Finally, agreements were made with the grape growers! Eventually, the union was renamed the United Farm Workers.
Fourth Picket Sign	End the Use of Pesticides
	Workers, many of them children, were exposed to pesticides sprayed on crops. Many forms of cancer, childhood leukemia, birth defects, injuries, and burns were the result of this exposure.
Narrator	Because of the efforts of Cesar and others, Californians passed laws to help farm workers. However, Cesar still had work to do. He was especially worried about poisons, or pesticides, sprayed on crops to control insects. These were a very great danger to farm workers. To draw attention to this issue, Cesar once again went on a food fast, this time for thirty-six days. Cesar continued his nonviolent fight for the rights of farm workers until he died in 1993. He believed in the dignity of work, and in the safety and rights of workers. Cesar spent his life working for both.

Discussion Starters

- After discussing the principle, talk about different working conditions. Recall the situations of child labor from the story about Free the Children.

- Explain to your children what a strike is and why workers might call one. Also explain why others might oppose them.

- What can you and your children do to help protect the rights of workers?

Suggestions for Finding this Theme in Children's Literature

Picture Books

Beatrice's Goat by Page McBrier

Wednesday's Surprise by Eve Bunting

A Day's Work by Eve Bunting

Jeremiah Learns to Read by Jo Ellen Bogart

My Rows and Piles of Coins by Tolowa M. Mollel

Early Chapter Books

Meet Samantha, An American Girl by Valerie Tripp

Chapter Books

Where the Red Fern Grows by Wilson Rawls

Jacob Have I Loved by Katherine Paterson

True Confessions of Charlotte Doyle by Avi

Dreams in a Golden Country, The Diary of Zipporah Feldman, a Jewish Immigrant Girl by Kathryn Lasky (Dear America series)

The Message of Silent Spring

A Story of Rachel Carson

The Principle

Perhaps the principle children will be most familiar with in Catholic social teaching is one concerning the environment. They have often heard about such issues as pollution and conservation. In the context of Catholic belief, they can begin to see this call to stewardship in spiritual terms.

God asks us to care for the magnificent creation we call earth. This is both a great privilege and a great responsibility. The earth supports us in life—it is our only support. Therefore, a troubled environment leads to significant justice issues. Pope John Paul II has called us as global citizens to respect life and to seek solutions together to our ecological problems.

The Story

In 1962, a quiet woman named Rachel Carson heeded the call to good stewardship by writing a book, *Silent Spring*, that instigated worldwide concern for preserving our environment. This is her story. Begin by having one person read the prayer based on Psalm 8 aloud, and end the story by praying the psalm together. You will need eight readers for this story.

Reader One	As a child, Rachel Carson loved to wander with her dog Candy over the sixty-five wooded acres in Pennsylvania that her family owned. She found baby robins and stopped to watch busy ants. Butterflies delighted her, as did the chirping of crickets and the singing of birds.
Reader Two	Rachel loved school. Sometimes, though, especially in bad weather, she stayed home and her mother taught her. They both loved science and nature. If Rachel had questions about life outside, her mother helped her find the answers. There was one other thing that Rachel loved: the ocean! She lived far away from it, but she longed to see it some day.
Reader Three	Long before Rachel was born, Pennsylvania was covered with great forests. There were bears, otters, beavers, and elk. But then people dug mines for coal. Forests were cut down so factories for steel and iron could be built. This caused rivers to become polluted. Most people accepted these changes as necessary. But Rachel's mother watched with sadness. She was glad her daughter was growing up on their beautiful land.

Reader Four	Rachel went to college, which was unusual for girls back then. She studied what she loved best, writing and science. Because she loved the sea, Rachel became a marine biologist. She worked for the Fish and Wildlife Service. Rachel wrote books like *Under the Sea Wind*, *The Sea Around Us*, and *The Edge of the Sea*. People said she made science sound like poetry. Rachel was asked to give many speeches.
Reader Five	In the 1940s and 1950s, terrible things were happening. Radioactive ashes from test bombs lingered in the air and ground. Sealed containers of nuclear waste were dumped into the ocean. Sewage and garbage were thrown into rivers. Carbon monoxide fumes from buses, trucks, and cars filled the air and people's lungs. Farmers, gardeners, foresters, and homeowners were now using dangerous chemicals like DDT for pest control. The companies who made the chemicals claimed they were safe, and the government agreed.
Reader Six	Only a few scientists like Rachel knew that fish were dying in polluted rivers. People who got the poisons on their skin often died. Rachel knew that small animals and whole forests died when chemicals were used widely.
	Rachel understood that if this continued, the poisons could end all life on earth. When spring time came, it would be silent. There would be no bird song, for there would be no birds or any people to appreciate it, either. She knew she must warn people. After much careful research, Rachel published her book, *Silent Spring*.
Reader Seven	Readers of *Silent Spring* were shocked and frightened. They wrote thousands of angry letters to newspapers, chemical companies, and the government. The chemical companies argued and tried to prove that Rachel was wrong. President Kennedy called for a special report to see who was right. The report showed that Rachel was right. New laws were made to limit pollution.
Reader Eight	Rachel was sick with cancer while *Silent Spring* was arousing all this interest, anger, and action. She died about a year later. The little girl who wandered the woods, wrote stories, and dreamed of the sea became the woman who awakened the world to preserve the environment. Our world is safer now because of her. Her spirit must live on in others, for there is still much work to do to care for God's creation, our earth.

Prayer of the People and the Earth

Based on Psalm 8

Leader	Let us pray.
Right Side	O Lord, our God, how awesome is your name through all the earth!
Left Side	When we see your heavens, the work of your hands, the moon and stars that you have set in place, we feel your greatness.
Right Side	We ask ourselves: what are we that God should love us so much?
Left Side	Yet, you have made us great and you have given us glory and honor.
Right Side	You want us to take care of all that you have created, all the sheep and oxen, and even the beasts of the field.
Left Side	You want us to watch over the birds of the air and the fish of the sea.
All	O Lord, our God, how awesome is your name through all the earth!

Discussion Starters

- Define the word "stewardship" and ask children what it means to be a steward of the earth.

- Help them see that their own actions have repercussions What do they do each day to preserve or renew the environment? What do they do daily that diminishes it? What decisions will they make eventually that will affect the earth (job choices, housing, transportation, etc.)?

- Then move to a broader discussion. How does the misuse of natural resources lead to poverty and suffering for many people? As Catholics called to stewardship, what role can students play in environmental issues?

Suggestions for Finding this Theme in Children's Literature

Picture Books

Forest of Dreams by Rosemary Wells
Old Turtle by Douglas Wood
Owl Moon by Jane Yolan
The Lorax by Dr. Seuss
In Every Tiny Grain of Sand: A Child's Book of Prayers and Praise by Reeve Lindbergh

Chapter Books

There's an Owl in the Shower by Jean Craighead George
Who Really Killed Cock Robin? by Jean Craighead George
My Side of the Mountain trilogy by Jean Craighead George
The Island by Gary Paulsen
Rascal by Sterling North
The House of Wings by Betsy Byers

We Are One Family
A Story of Children in Today's World

The Principle

If we adhere to the previous six principles, we come naturally to the next one: we are called to love each other. We must see ourselves as one human family, whatever our national, racial, ethnic, economic, or ideological differences. We are indeed our brothers' and sisters' keepers. We are all linked to one another. When there is violent conflict or when people are denied their rights and dignity in any part of the world, it diminishes us all. Therefore, seeking and demanding justice for our neighbor must take on worldwide dimensions.

The Story

Well-known people, like Pope John Paul II and Nelson Mandela, are working for unity among the world's peoples. Many others, lesser known, such as missionaries, medical workers, teachers, government workers, and community organizers, strive for solidarity too. This important task will be passed on to the next generation, so it is imperative that children see their own connections—their solidarity—with others in the world. The following story includes brief descriptions of the lives of ten different children. After discussing the principle, draw a large circle with chalk on the floor, explaining that this will represent the world. Choose ten readers for the story. After each one reads his/her part, the reader then enters the circle, facing outward. They should stand near the chalk line so, as readers enter, they will form a circle within the circle. In addition, choose a narrator who can read Scripture well. This person should stand apart from the circle for the readings.

Narrator	In the first letter to the Corinthians, chapter 12, Saint Paul teaches that we are all important. He does this by comparing the peoples of God's world to the human body. The body has many parts that work together. He writes, "The body is not a single part, but many. If a foot should say, 'Because I am not a hand I do not belong to the body,' it does not...belong any less to the body." Now we will listen to the voices of children who help make up God's world.
Reader One	I am twelve years old, and I live in an orphanage in Siberia. I am grateful that Catholic people in Austria and Poland sent money so our orphanage could buy 190 pairs of boots and 450 pounds of apples!
Reader Two	My twin brother and I are eight years old. We live in El Salvador, and we love

	to visit our neighbor. She is ninety years old! We bring her water for washing. We fetch kindling so she can build a fire for cooking. Often, we play cards with her.
Reader Three	I am a girl living in the countryside of Nepal. Thanks to a school started by Christian missionaries, I am learning to read and write. Most likely my father will choose a husband for me by the time I am ten years old. But I hope I can go on learning, too.
Reader Four	When I was about four years old, my family had to flee from violence in our country of Burundi to our neighbor country of Tanzania. Each day we receive corn and beans from the United Nations food program. Everywhere you look, people have gardens. It is very crowded, but some adults built a church from trees and plastic sheeting. Sometimes, we play soccer. Mostly, it seems, we wait to see it if will be safe for us to go home. Now I don't remember what home is like any more.
Reader Five	I live high in the mountains of Viet Nam. My family has a water buffalo to pull the plows in the fields. I love to ride on its back!
Narrator	Saint Paul continues to tell us how people must work together. He still uses the example of the human body: "There are many parts, yet one body. The eye cannot say to the hand, 'I do not need you.'"
Reader Six	I am six years old. I survived Hurricane Mitch which greatly damaged my country of Honduras. My home and everything we owned were washed away. We had nothing left, but we are alive! Now we live in a makeshift shelter my father built. Today some people brought us mattresses. We will sleep well tonight!
Reader Seven	I am a fifth grader in the midwestern United States. I have one sister and one brother, and we each have our own bedroom. I take horse-riding lessons and piano lessons. Every Wednesday night, I attend religion classes at my church. Also I like to read. Mysteries are my favorites!
Reader Eight	I live in Jordan, and I am nine years old. When it is the month of Ramadan, we Muslims fast between sunrise and sunset. We pray each day, wearing special clothes at prayer time. At the end of our month of fasting, we celebrate with three days of feasting. We visit relatives and friends and exchange gifts. That is a happy time each year!
Reader Nine	I live in northern Thailand; I am one of the Ahha people. Our village lies in the mountains. One of my favorite things is when the missioner priest arrives at our church. We all rush to him, and as is our custom, each of us greets him. No matter how young or old you are, you get a turn. First you press your palms together and bow your head. Then you stand tall and hold out your right arm, holding this arm up at the elbow with your left hand. Then you grasp his hand. The priest is much taller than I am, so I really stand tall to greet him!

Reader Ten	I am seven years old. I live in Seoul, in the Republic of Korea, or South Korea. It is a city of tall, modern buildings and beautiful ancient palaces. I live with my family in a small apartment. At school we take our shoes off. Visitors are sometimes given plastic bags to put over their shoes! When I am a little older, I may take piano or violin lessons and English classes. For now, I love to skate!
Narrator	Saint Paul concludes, "God has so constructed the body...that there may be no division...but that the parts may have the same concern for one another. If (one) part suffers, all the parts suffer with it; if one part is honored, all the parts share its joy."
	Let's see one another as members of one family. Together let's work for justice for all of our brothers and sisters in the world.

Discussion Starters

Bring in the book, *Children Just Like Me* by Barnabas and Anabel Kindersley (Dorling Kindersley) before reading this story. This book can be found in public libraries. It is filled with appealing color photos, and celebrates intriguing differences and similarities of children in some thirty-five countries. The book can be read in small groups or individually.

After reading the story, discuss with your children:

- Do they see themselves as world citizens?

- Do they feel there are issues affecting other children that they could be involved in?

- Are there aspects of their lives that could be changed to benefit others?

- Consider adding a prayer to each class period, to recognize the unity among all peoples. Ask God for guidance in how to act on it.

Suggestions for Finding this Theme in Children's Literature

Picture Books
Smokey Night by Eve Bunting
Stone Soup by Marcia Brown, or other versions
The Turnip by Harriet Zieffert
We All Sing with the Same Voice by Philip Miller and Shepard Greene

Early Chapter Books
Twenty and Ten by Claire Huchet Bishop
Happy Birthday Molly, An American Girl by Valerie Tripp

Chapter Books
Fight in the Fields: Cesar Chavez by Margo Sorenson
Number the Stars by Lois Lowry
Jane Gibbs, Little Bird That Was Caught by Anne E. Neuberger

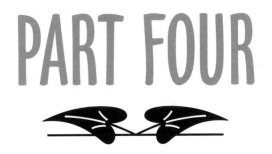

PART FOUR

Resources for Action

Books for Africa

Books for Africa has a simple mission: to collect, sort, ship, and distribute books to children in Africa. Their goal is to end the book famine there. Books are donated by publishers, schools, libraries, individuals, and organizations. They are sorted and packed by volunteers, and shipped in containers paid for by contributions. Since 1988, Books for Africa has shipped more than 6 million books, which have reached the hands of children who had never held books before.

Increasing numbers of American school children have responded by collecting books, school supplies, or money. Participating children have reported feeling a personal connection to students in African countries, a knowledge of the African continent and its issues, and a sense of accomplishment in completing a significant project. BFA welcomes any level of involvement.

> Website: www.booksforafrica.org
> Contact:
> Books for Africa
> 253 East 4th Street
> Saint Paul, MN 55101
> 651-602-9844
> FAX: 651-602-9848
> E-MAIL: info@booksforafrica.org

Bread for the World/Institute

Bread for the World is a nationwide Christian movement that seeks justice for the world's hungry people by lobbying our nation's decision makers. *Bread for the World Institute* also seeks justice by engaging in research and education on policies related to hunger and development.

> Website: www.bread.org

In addition to information on *Bread for the World* projects, this site provides links to other anti-hunger and poverty websites.

RESOURCES

For adults:

Grace at the Table: Ending Hunger in God's World, by David Beckman and Art Simon.

Hunger No More, materials to help Christians understand how we can work to end hunger.

Lazarus: A Musical on Hunger and Poverty, a full-length musical about hunger and poverty in the Bible and today.

For children

Make Hunger History, a booklet filled with a variety of creative activities to teach children about hunger issues.

> Contact: Bread for the World
> 50 F Street NW, Suite 500
> Washington, DC 20001
> 1-800-82-BREAD
> FAX 202-639-9401

Catholic Extension

Catholic Extension is the largest supporter of Catholic missionary work in the United States and its territories, allocating more than $16 million to needy dioceses each year.

Children can learn about missionaries working in places like Alaska, Appalachia, and Texas through a variety of free or low-cost offerings.

> Website www.catholic-extension.org

Their award-winning website offers more than 1000 Catholic links and has been a noted favorite for students hoping to enhance their research skills as well as their spirituality. On the site, register for a free subscription to *Extension* Magazine as well as the Weekly Meditation, words of saints and spiritual leaders arriving to you or your child's e-mail address every Monday morning.

Video: *Amazing Grace: An American Missionary Journal*

This engaging 15-minute video will take children through a day in the life of three American missionaries.

> Contact: Catholic Extension
> Communications Department
> 150 S. Wacker Drive, 20th Floor
> Chicago, Illinois 60606
> 1-888-473-2484

Catholic Relief Services

Catholic Relief Services was founded in 1943 by the Catholic bishops of the United States to assist poor and disadvantaged people outside the country. The fundamental motivating force in all activities of CRS is the gospel of Jesus Christ as it pertains to the alleviation of human suffering, the development of people, and the fostering of charity and justice in the world. But the world is a vastly different place today than it was in 1943. Founded to assist European refugees during World War II, CRS has, in the past five decades, served millions of the world's poor though emergency relief efforts and development programs. Relief and development work that will improve lives requires a focus on the social, economic, cultural, and political structures that either create or perpetrate the very conditions CRS addresses. It is not enough to engage in commendable service if there is no challenge to the social structures that continue to oppress and impoverish people.

Website www.catholicrelief.org

RESOURCES

Operation Rice Bowl

Operation Rice Bowl is CRS's lenten program which calls participants to pray, fast, learn, and give. Free resources are provided to bring a global dimension to these four components into the school, classroom, parish, and home. Stories and concrete activities bring the realities of the poor to life for children, and give suggestions about how to put faith into action. Age-appropriate lesson plans are provided in the Educator's Guide, and a Home Calendar Guide and Rice Bowl in the home will complement classroom teaching. Free materials are available through the website, www.catholicrelief.org/orb or by calling 800-222-0025.

Kids' Website

The CRS Kid's Site includes games and activities for children aged 8-13 to introduce them to life in various countries where CRS works. The topics covered there include issues about poverty, hunger, water, and refugees. Interactive games and activities share what life is like around the world and raises the awareness of what CRS is doing to assist. In particular, there is a Kid's Newsroom that updates youngsters on current situations around the world. Teachers will find lesson plans to integrate into classrooms as well. Visit www.catholicrelief.org/kids/index.html or go to the CRS homepage and click on the Kids' Site icon.

Catholic Social Teaching and Education Program

University of St. Thomas, Catholic Studies

The John A. Ryan Institute for Catholic Social Thought, St. Paul, Minnesota

This program serves as a support to teachers seeking to integrate Catholic social teaching into their curriculum. It offers courses, study groups, and lectures for ongoing theological education and formation of teachers at the elementary, secondary, and college levels. Serving as a clearinghouse for Catholic social teaching curriculum materials, this program works with teachers to create and distribute lesson plans and guides for CST pedagogy.

A website is being developed so that teachers throughout the country can access Catholic social teaching material and curriculum aids. It aims to serve as a resource for ongoing learning of Catholic social teaching and for the work of integrating Catholic social teaching across various disciplines.

Contact: Deborah Wallace Ruddy

Director, Catholic Social Teaching and Education

dwruddy@stthomas.edu

http://www.stthomas.edu/cathstudies/cst/educ/

Christian Foundation for Children and Aging

Christian Foundation for Children and Aging was founded by Catholic laypersons as a way to help the poor and to build friendships between people of different cultures. CFCA helps children and aging persons in 25 countries with education, nutrition, medical care, clothing, and other needs. The organization provides opportunities for Catholics to act on the Church's social teaching, and to form friendships across borders through prayer and correspondence. CFCA works with lay organizations, missionary orders, and the local Catholic Church at more than 100 coordinating centers and 2,200 mission sites abroad.

CFCA has many opportunities for adults, and children's involvement. Among them are:

- Read about children from other countries in *Sacred Ground*, CFCA's newsletter, which is mailed to sponsors three times a year and is available online.

- Sponsor a needy child or aging person in one of the Latin American, Asian, or African countries where CFCA works.

- Sponsor a vocation candidate studying for the priesthood or religious life.

- Donate to a scholarship fund to help needy students pursue education through college or vocational training.

- Visit the missions on a CFCA Missions Awareness Trip.

- Volunteer in the missions or Kansas City headquarters.

- Invite a priest representing CFCA to your parish to celebrate weekend Masses and to talk about CFCA's work.

- Host a CFCA Sponsorship Party, and invite friends and family to sponsor a needy child or aging person.

- Talk to a religion class or youth group about how CFCA helps the poor.

> Contact: Christian Foundation for Children and Aging
> One Elmwood Avenue
> Kansas City, Kansas 66103
> 1-800-875-6564
> e-mail mail@cfcausa.org
> Website www.cfcausa.org

Church World Service

Church World Service is a ministry of 36 Protestant, Anglican, and Orthodox communions in the United States. In partnership with indigenous organizations in more than 80 countries, CWS supports self-help development, meets emergency needs, and helps address the root causes of poverty and powerlessness. Within the United States, CWS assists communities with disaster relief and resettlement of refugees, promotes fair national and international policies, and offers opportunities to join a people-to-people network of local and global caring through participation in Crops Walk, Tools of Hope and Blanket Program, and Gift of the Heart kits program.

RESOURCES

Film and Video Library

CWS operates a free-loan audio-visual library. To receive a brochure listing audiovisual selections on hunger, social justice, and related issues, e-mail to cws.film.library@ecunet.org or use the information listed below.

Publications

Build a Better World! Activities for Children from Church World Service. Four Journeys (Ghana, Around the Block, Honduras, and Cambodia) for elementary school children.
We Can Do That, Too! Hunger Education Activities that Work. For all ages.

> Contact: 1-800-297-1516

Church World Service
P.O. Box 968
Elkhart, IN 46515

Claretian Publications

This Catholic publisher, funded by the Claretian Fathers, offers several resources on current social justice topics that are helpful for adults working with children.

Website: www.claretianpubs.org

This site offers information on their publications as well as *Salt of the Earth*, an online resource for social justice issues, and *The Busy Christian's Guide to Catholic Social Teachings*. In addition, you can link with many other websites on a wide variety of topics such as homelessness, peace, human rights, hunger, labor, and Catholic volunteerism.

The Columbans

The Columbans are a missionary society serving God's people in the contemporary world. Founded in 1918 as St. Columban's Foreign Mission Society, they minister to their brothers and sisters in other lands and cultures. Their special role lies in crossing boundaries of language, culture, and faith to bring the gospel to others. Over 700 Columbans minister in 17 countries, especially to the poor and victims of injustice. In the United States, they assist Catholics in understanding the missionary call of their faith, and to act as agents between God's people overseas and their brothers and sisters in the United States.

The Columbans cooperate with other mission-sending groups in this common task. All their mission awareness resource materials are offered as part of their service to the church in the United States.

RESOURCES

Video Programs

Vinny's New Day, for preschool and kindergarten. Vinny the Toucan introduces students to children of other lands. Children learn about baptism and belonging to the family of God, about missioners and being called to love like Jesus. Complete with manual, video, and CD. Free loan for 21 days.

Come and See, for K through 8. Five-lesson format that introduces students to children of other lands. Each grade level has a different theme. Students will come to see how special and unique all children are, and celebrate the similarities and differences. Complete with manual, video, wall charts and gifts for each student.

Contact:
Mission Education Office
Columban Fathers
P.O. Box 10
St. Columbans, NE 68056-9901
402-291-1920
FAX: 402-291-4984
Website: st.columban.org/missioned

Free the Children

Free the Children is an international network of children helping children, and was founded by children. It works to free children from poverty, exploitation, and abuse, and to give children leadership training and opportunities to take action on many levels. (See the story about this organization, *Children Freeing Children: A Story of Craig Kielburger*, in Part Three.)

Website: www.freethechildren.com

RESOURCES

Take Action! A Guide to Active Citizenship (Gage Learning), a how-to guide to social involvement geared to students and teachers.

Free the Children by Craig Kielburger with Kevin Major (HarperCollins).

Heifer Project International

Since 1944, Heifer International has helped more than 4 million families become self-reliant by providing them with "living loans" of livestock. Currently, Heifer supports over 300 projects in 47 countries to create sustainable, small-scale farm enterprises that help families lift themselves out of poverty. Not only are families trained in proper care and maintenance of these animals, but they are also required to "pass on the gift" by giving one or more of their animal's offspring to another family in need. Heifer International offers children numerous opportunities to learn about the need for social justice and to work for it:

Website: www.heifer.org

RESOURCES

Read to Feed This program motivates school children to read books so they can help hungry children all over the world. Students in kindergarten through sixth grade learn about other cultures, world hunger, the environment, and how communities work together to become self-reliant. They may also learn the games, songs, stories and food of children in other countries. The children ask their families and friends to sponsor them for each book they read to raise money which is sent to Heifer International, which will benefit farm animal projects in the United States and other countries.

Fill the Ark This program uses a four-week calendar which describes the animals in Heifer's "Ark" that help hungry people become self-sufficient, and an ark-shaped bank. As participants fill the bank with coins, they meet the alpaca, bee, camel, chicken, cow, donkey, duck, fish, goose, guinea pig, horse, llama, pig, rabbit, sheep, water buffalo and yak, learn how these animals help families, and the environmental benefits of managing animals wisely. Included are the calendars and banks, a Leader's Guide with homily notes, children's activities, and creative worship ideas.

Animal Crackers, Ages 3 to Adult

This five-session program, divided by age groups, explores the topics of:

• hunger and the Bible
• animals
• people and their needs
• the environment
• passing on the gift

This is designed to enhance summer and school year religious education programs. Animal Crackers allows students to raise money for donation of a animal to a struggling family. The guidebook includes learning sessions, world hunger facts, animal fact sheets and activities, Bible passages and games.

Book: *Beatrice's Goat*, by Page McBrier and Lori Lohstoeter. This children's picture book is based on the true story of nine-year-old Ugandan girl whose family was given a dairy goat by Heifer Project International. Published by Simon and Schuster.

Other opportunities: Heifer International has three Learning Centers, hands-on campuses that teach the public about world hunger, and study tours which take participants for one or two weeks to visit and work on Heifer projects in the United States and other countries.

Contact: Heifer Project International
1015 Louisiana Street
Little Rock, AR 72202
800-696-1918

Humphrey, Sandra McLeod, Author

Books:

• *If You Had to Choose, What Would You Do?*, for ages 6-12.

• *It's Up to You...What Do You Do?*, for ages 8 and up.

Both are interactive books about moral choices which help guide children through everyday problems and instill a sense of responsibility for their own choices. Both books contain 25 stories involving making a moral choice. Questions follow each story to facilitate discussions for both home and school use. These books can be ordered through any major bookstore, on the internet, or through Prometheus Books at 1-800-421-0351.

Website: www.kidscandoit.com

Instructional Services Center (ISC)

The *Jeff Johnson Instructional Services Center* is a media lending library of the Archdiocese of St. Paul and Minneapolis. Its 3000 videos are available for use by any individual, church, or school. The collection includes videos for preschoolers through adults in English and Spanish.

Contact: 1-800-303-2336
E-mail: blenkushm@archspm.org

Kids Can Make a Difference

Kids Can Make a Difference ® (KIDS), a program of World Hunger Year (WHY), is an innovative educational program for middle-school and high-school students. It helps them understand the root causes of hunger and poverty, and how they can take action. The program includes:

• "Finding Solutions to Hunger: Kids Can Make a Difference" teacher guide, by Stephanie Kempf. This book is a wealth of resources, listing many books and videos for children and adults on topics such as work, war, hunger, homelessness, slavery, racism and resistance, education in third world countries, the plight of refugees, child labor.

• An award-winning website: www.kidscanmakeadifference.org

• A newsletter that highlights current hunger issues, student initiatives, and teachers' experiences in teaching about hunger.

Contact: kids@kidscanmakeadifference.org
207-439-9588

Maryknoll Missioners

Founded in 1911, Maryknoll today consists of more than 1,500 priests, brothers, sisters, and lay missioners serving in 37 countries around the world. Called to share their faith in Jesus, they discover new faces of God among people of different racial, religious, and ethnic backgrounds. Following the gospel, these missioners are dedicated to building a better world of holiness, justice, and peace through the many ways they serve others.

Website: www.maryknoll.org

This site offers a wealth of information and includes games and challenges for children.

RESOURCES

Videos

• *The Field Afar* A 17-part video series with study guides and educator notes. Each 22-minute video focuses on a country, its problems, some solutions, and the beauty there; some titles are Mexico, Peru, Thailand, Bangladesh, Tanzania, Panama, the Philippines, and Mozambique.

• *Children of the Earth* These eight videos are available in English and Spanish and Closed Caption, and include study guides. Each video presents two different places (i.e. Peru and Brazil) and introduces children (mostly ages 13 and 14) in their everyday lives. In addition to these videos, there are many more on world cultures and religions, child labor, young women's issues, hunger, etc.

Posters

Laminated posters are offered for Advent, Stations of the Cross, Sacraments, and the Beatitudes.

Coloring and Activity Book

This 24-page book has stories, facts, maps, illustrations to color, and puzzles about Peru, the Philippines, Kenya, and Guatemala.

Magazines

Maryknoll Magazine Classroom Program includes magazines, posters, and teacher's guides. For specific information on this, call 1-800-558-2292 ex. 183.

Contact: Maryknoll World Productions
PO Box 308
Maryknoll, NY 10545-0308
800-227-8523
FAX: 914-762-6567

The Office for Social Justice, Archdiocese of St. Paul and Minneapolis

The Office for Social Justice in the Archdiocese of St. Paul and Minneapolis educates Catholics about the Church's rich social teaching and provides Catholics with opportunities to act on this teaching in the public arena.

Website: www.osjspm.org

This website features links to all the social encyclicals written in the past 100 years, several pastoral letters released by the U.S. bishops, and other sites related to Catholic social teaching. In addition, quotations from the Church's teaching have been organized by topic, and there are links that include stories about successful efforts to educate young people about Catholic social teaching.

The Poverty Project

The Poverty Project is a teacher resource written by educator Linda Hanson. It takes young people out of the world of textbooks and into the world of life decisions, simulation experiences, as well as research into conditions of local poverty. The Project focuses on the Catholic social teaching, "Option for the Poor and Vulnerable." This cross-curriculum unit of study involves math, religion, social studies, literature, language, and technology. It can easily be applied in Christian formation programs, confirmation preparation, or as a unit in a day school for grades 6-12. In accordance with Catholic social teaching, it challenges the students to measure their society by how it treats the least among them. The Poverty Project is published by the Sisters of St. Joseph of Carondolet.

> Contact: Good Ground Press
> 1884 Randolph Ave.
> St. Paul, MN 55105
> 1-800-232-5533

Sisters of the Blessed Sacrament

Sister Katharine Drexel left a home of great wealth and luxury for a life of service. As a young woman, she began to support missionaries and schools in the United States and abroad. In 1889, she entered religious life, and in 1891, Mother Katharine founded a religious order of women dedicated to educating and sharing the Catholic faith with the Native and African American peoples. She worked for social justice for those who were often neglected or abused by their government and neighbors. Today, the Sisters of the Blessed Sacrament continue St. Katharine's vision by promoting education and by working for social justice among the poor and neglected peoples of the United States, Haiti, and Guatemala. (See the story of Katharine Drexel in Part I.)

Web site: www.katharinedrexel.org

RESOURCES

Books:

For Adults

Katharine Drexel A Biography by Sister Consuela Marie Duffy, SBS

Sharing the Bread in Service: Sisters of the Blessed Sacrament, 1891-1991 by Sister Patricia Lynch, SBS

For Young Readers

Katharine Drexel: Friend of the Oppressed by Ellen Tarry

Kate from Philadelphia: The Life of Saint Katharine Drexel for Children by Patricia Edward Jablonski, FSP, illustrated by Mary Julius Hausmann, SBS. This is a comic book format, easily read and well done. There is also a coloring book featuring the artist's illustrations.

These titles are available through their website, or through the Peacemaker, a publication of the Sisters of the Blessed Sacrament.

> Contact: Peacemaker
> 1663 Bristol Pike
> Bensalem, PA 19020-5796
> Anyone wishing to do further research can contact:
> Stephanie Morris, Ph.D., Director of Archives,
> 215-244-9900 ex. 352

United States Conference of Catholic Bishops (USCCB)

The United States Conference of Catholic Bishops is a group of all the bishops of the Catholic Church in the United States and Virgin Islands. They work together to help Catholics understand Jesus better and to learn how to live more like him. The bishops write on many important subjects like peace and violence, Africa, immigrants and refugees. USCCB Publishing prints many of the statements that the bishops write and is the official publisher of the U.S. Catholic bishops.

RESOURCES

Publications

• *In All Things Charity: A Pastoral Challenge for the New Millennium.* The bishops challenge all people of faith to engage in acts of·charity and to undertake action to promote justice and peace. Available in both English and Spanish.

• *Principles, Prophecy, and a Pastoral Response.* Highlighting the seven themes of Catholic social teaching, this booklet includes excerpts from papal encyclicals and bishops' pastoral letters, and examples of how to implement the basic themes. Available in both English and Spanish.

• *Sharing Catholic Social Teaching: Challenges and Directions.* Stresses the importance of and explores ways of incorporating Catholic social teaching into Catholic educational programs. Available in both English and Spanish.

For children, grades 2-6:

Cards and posters: Excerpts from *Sharing Catholic Social Teaching.* These highlight the seven themes of Catholic social teaching. Available in both English and Spanish.

Videos:

• *The Richest Dog in the World.* This 10-minute video presents, in animated form, the challenges of the world's poor, aid imbalance, interdependence, empowering the poor, limits to growth.

• *The Mouse's Tale.* This 11-minute cartoon explores the issues of international food production and its relationship to hunger and famine.

Contact: USCCB Publishing

1-800-235-8722 or 202-541-3090

Fax: 202-541-3089

Website: www.usccb.org

E-mail: publications@usccb.org